Flowing Wealth

Flowing Wealth

Exceedingly
abundantly
above all that
we can ask or think

by
David S. Wells III
and
Suzie Wells

Harrison House
Tulsa, Oklahoma

Unless otherwise indicated, all Scripture quotations are taken from the *King James Version* of the Bible.

All Scripture quotations marked NIV are taken from *The Holy Bible: New International Version.* Copyright © 1973, 1978, 1984 by The International Bible Society. Used by permission of Zondervan Bible Publishers.

Scripture quotations taken from *The Amplified Bible, Old Testament,* copyright © 1964, 1987 by The Zondervan Corporation, Grand Rapids, Michigan, *The Amplified Bible, New Testament,* copyright © 1958, 1987 by The Lockman Foundation, La Habra, California, are used by permission.

AP is used to indicate "Author's Paraphrase."

Flowing Wealth
ISBN 0-89274-917-2
Copyright © 1995
by David Sloan Wells III
and Linda Diane (Suzie) Wells
P.O. Box 5646
Abilene, TX 79608

Published by Harrison House, Inc.
P.O. Box 35035
Tulsa, Oklahoma 74153

Contents

Acknowledgments

Dr. Harrison and the books of Harrison House have stabilized, energized, educated and safely guided Suzie and me since the early 70s. Where would we be without the enlightenment of God's Word in these great books which Dr. Harrison releases to the world? Thank you, Dr. Harrison and Pat, for your faithfulness to feed us and the world with God's pure Word through Harrison House books. Your faithfulness has laid the foundation for the truths we personally now have for the Body of Christ. Thank you for helping us share them now with the world through Harrison House.

Our deepest thanks also to Editorial Director, Cris Boley, for her professional, spiritual and personal attention to *Flowing Wealth*. We are so grateful that she has perfected our book with her unique combination of spiritual and editorial skills.

David S. Wells III
October 21, 1994

Dedication

This book is dedicated in appreciation to:

- Our steadfast partners and associates of Redeeming Love Faith Fellowship Church, who have joyfully received these Flowing Wealth principles, are succesfully applying them and have supportively insisted that we put these principles into print.

- Our three fine sons, David, Christian and Caleb who have enthusiastically shared in our years of dedication to the charity principle—yet, are now experiencing the exciting benefits of God's Plan of Flowing Wealth, which gives the hand of charity a bounty of greater supply.

Foreword

In today's society there is great confusion about money and wealth. You understand that in the world, but it shouldn't be that way in the church. And yet, it is just as confusing there as anywhere else.

David Wells' book, *Flowing Wealth*, brings to the body of Christ great understanding of principles that must be operative in our lives for us to be what we ought to be. God owns everything, the world and the fullness thereof, but He entrusted it to men. And how faithful men are in their stewardship with what is given to them is of utmost importance.

I love the things that David brings out relative to Joseph, and the parables and all the different lessons that there are to learn. One of the important things to understand is that money does move and that as long as money is moving, it can purify. Just as water flowing so far will purify itself, so money moving in the kingdom of God will purify and bring honor unto God.

Money moves from nation to nation, from person to person. When money, just as water, quits flowing, it stagnates. And it will become rottenness to a man's bones.

So, you need to understand flowing wealth, and David does a wonderful job of sharing these truths. I encourage you, take advantage of the knowledge that is here. Underline these truths, implement them into your life, for they will bring great blessing. As David has been a blessing to me personally, through the truths that he has brought, I want these truths from this book to be a blessing to you.

God bless you,
Buddy Harrison
Founder of Harrison House

Introduction

This book is dedicated to the liberation of every human being from the pain and destruction of lack in a world filled with abundance. Each individual has a God-given right to walk in the abundance this earth has to offer. The principles in this book will teach you why God wants you to prosper and how to gain abundant wealth for use in God's kingdom.

When properly used, the mysterious unseen force of a magnet draws objects to it and forcefully holds them. When improperly used, the magnet repells objects. The principles of God's Plan for Flowing Wealth work the same way. Apply His simple principles correctly and wealth will flow to you as mysteriously as the unseen force of a magnet draws objects to it. Violate these principles and wealth is repelled.

The teaching presented here contains the same principles Jesus taught 2,000 years ago. Even so, only a few of His followers have ever completely applied them. Most believers have applied only a portion of God's Plan for Flowing Wealth and have never enjoyed the prosperity God intended for them to have.

Joseph used these principles 1,500 years before the birth of Christ to feed the world and provide a healthy world market—during the worst famine the world had known, which lasted seven years.

These are the same wealth-drawing keys a distraught minister's wife used 2,600 years ago, when her husband died and the creditors came to put her sons in debtors' prison. She began to use the one key she had not been applying. Immediately, she began to experience wealth flowing to her—when in the past it was repelled. She and her sons were able to pay their debts in just a matter of days. By beginning to operate one principle she had missed, wealth flowed to this widow.

These keys are for you. They are from God, who loves you so much He put you on a planet of abundance and gave you the keys to guarantee you have your abundant share. Apply His simple formula of pulling wealth to you, and your abundant share of the world's wealth will flow to you.

This book will show you:

- How to have abundant flowing wealth.
- How to never lose wealth and increase it.
- How to recover more than you have lost.
- How to maintain wealth.
- How to enjoy wealth.
- How to do good with the wealth God intends for you to have.

Apply the simple keys of this book and your name will be remembered for philanthropy, not poverty.

David S. Wells III

1
God's Divine Plan for Flowing Wealth

He will bless those who reverently and worshipfully fear the Lord, both small and great.

The Lord give you increase more and more, you and your children.

Blessed be you of the Lord, Who made heaven and earth!

The heavens are the Lord's heavens, *but the earth has He given to the children of men.*

Psalm 115:13-16 AMP

God has an unfailing plan to bless His people so they will consistently increase from the unlimited riches He has put into the earth. Jesus clearly teaches in Matthew 25:31-46 that He will return to earth from heaven and call His people, the sheep of His pasture, to inherit the kingdom that has been prepared for them from the foundation of the world.

Those who will inherit this promise will be those who gave Jesus meat when He was hungry, drink when He was thirsty, a place to stay when He was a stranger, clothing when He was naked, visited Him when He was sick and went to Him when He was in prison. And many will ask, "Lord, when did we see You hungry and feed You, or thirsty and give You something to drink? When did we give You clothes or visit You when You were sick or in prison?"

Jesus will answer and say, **Inasmuch as ye have done it unto one of the least of these my brethren, ye have done it unto me** (Matt. 25:40).

The Consequence of Unbelief

Jesus illustrates in Matthew, chapter 25, that there will be a separation between those who give and those who do not give to others. It will be as a separation of goats from sheep. If our Lord places such a dramatic importance on giving, then we can trust Him to provide what we need to fulfill this command to give.

Yet many Christians are so greatly in debt, they are not able to provide for their own family, let alone for the needs of strangers. Many Christians remain poor because they do not believe in God's plan of prosperity for His children, but most Christians are poor because they do not know or understand the principles of God's Plan for Flowing Wealth found in the Word of God.

The children of Israel learned that there is a consequence to doubting the Word of God. They paid a heavy price for this sin by refusing to enter into the Promised Land when God wanted them to because of their unbelief. (Heb. 3:7-16.) There is also a consequence for those who doubt that God wants His people to be givers—eternal separation from God. Matthew 25:46 reveals this in Jesus' own words: **And these** [who did not minister to those in need] **shall go away into everlasting punishment: but the righteous into life eternal.**

God will equip us for what He has called us to do. When we see that we are to give in His name, we can expect Him to provide the wealth that is needed to give. *Jesus clearly teaches how and that we are to gain wealth for His use* in the parable of the talents, found in this same chapter of Matthew 25. We will examine this parable more closely in chapter 3 of this book. I refer to the lesson taught in this parable as the Gaining and Giving Principles for financing the ministry of God's people throughout the earth. When you apply this unfailing financial plan of Jesus, His unlimited power of giving will flow through you. Riches you did not dream were possible will be in your personal possession to fulfill His ministry on earth.

But before we look more closely at how to acquire wealth for God's purposes, let's investigate this inheritance that has been planned for us since the creation of the world. (Matt. 25:34.)

Adam Was to Rule Over the Vast Wealth of God

In the beginning God planned for man to subdue the earth and rule over all other living creatures. Adam was placed over the vast wealth of the garden of Eden, which was pulsating with the uncontaminated purity of riches. Genesis 2:11 says the gold of that land was good, and there was bdellium (aromatic resin or fragrant gum) and onyx. Everything was "very good" and was placed under man's control. (Gen. 1:26, 2:15.)

God placed His son Adam (Luke 3:38) in the rich garden to dress and keep it. Adam was then commanded to freely partake of everything in the garden, except the one forbidden tree. God didn't just invite Adam to enjoy the fruit of the garden. He commanded Adam to freely eat of every tree that was pleasant to his taste, except the tree of the knowledge of good and evil. *Adam was to stay away from the tree that represented disobedience to God.*

Deception Caused Man to Lose God's Prosperity Plan

Satan's first attempt to deceive was by corrupting man's understanding of God's Plan of Flowing Wealth for him. God had given Adam everything in the garden for his use except one tree—the tree that would separate man from God.

Prosperity was freely available for Adam through his fellowship with the Father. Fellowship with the Father included an intimate knowledge of His will and abundant provision for the needs of man. To remain in this prosperous state of fellowship, Adam was to obey the exact instructions the Father had given him.

Satan polluted Adam's understanding of God's provision by attacking the purity of God's Word. Satan tempted Adam to doubt the promises of God and to therefore willfully disobey what he knew God had said. The consequence of disobedience caused Adam to lose the abundant provision of God. (Gen. 3:23.)

God had to send Adam away from Eden to keep him from eating from the tree of life, thus remaining in a fallen state forever. Satan temporarily stripped man of his fellowship with God and of his inheritance of God's flowing wealth for man.

Since Satan's first attack on man was against the intimate relationship he had with the Father and the consequent prosperity He had given to man, it must have been the greatest threat to Satan. Satan fights what hurts him most. Satan's first attack was to cause man to question the integrity of God's Word.

Today Satan continues to attack the purity of God's Word and deceives us into thinking that God does not really mean exactly what He has said. God has promised abundant life through trusting Jesus Christ as our Savior. Satan's desire is to kill and destroy, which is far from abundant, but Jesus has come that we might have life, and have it to the fullest. (John 10:10.)

If Satan can convince Christians to believe it is spiritual to be poor and sick, then the church will not flow in the abundant provision of God's wealth needed to carry the Good News of Jesus Christ to all people. Doubt and unbelief in God's promises will keep His blessings from flowing freely.

Satan knows that Christians will not have the ability to set humanity free if their physical strength is diminished and if they lack the finances to feed the hungry, clothe the naked, visit the sick, shelter the homeless and preach the Gospel. Satan wants to keep Christians in a state of poverty and unbelief to keep us from presenting the Good News to our community and world. Satan still tempts us to disobey God by doubting the purity of His Word.

Is It Spiritual to Be Poor and Sick?

Many Christians believe it is God's will for them to be very limited materially in order for them to be more spiritual. Others argue that God allows sickness in order to teach a spiritual lesson. However, if we become more spiritual through poverty and illness, then "superspiritual" people could not fulfill Jesus' command to go and tell the world the Good News of His Gospel. They would not have the health or finances to reach others. God would have to depend on the more "carnal" (healthy and wealthy) Christians to spread the Gospel, because the "really spiritual" believers would be too poor and too sick to go! The poor and sick Christians would *desire* to go and tell others of God's Good News, but they would lack the *ability* to go.

If sickness and poverty glorify God, then it would be carnal to be healthy and without needs. If it glorifies God to be poor and sick, we would have to pray, "God, let us be carnal enough to have the health and wealth to go tell the world about Jesus."

God doesn't use sin to advance righteousness. He uses righteousness to abolish sin.

If sickness and poverty build character, then don't pray for healing and finances to carry the Good News of Jesus! To do so would mean you were praying for a measure of sin to carry out God's will in your life.

By this standard, to be totally spiritual you would have to be dead! The process of sickness ultimately leads to death. But again, sickness which leads you to death puts you in an impossible position to be the witness God has called you to be. Death would put you in heaven, and He has not asked you to witness there. He has asked you to be a witness on the earth. But if you continue to believe God wants you to be sick, you will have to dedicate your life to the pursuit of dying in order to be totally spiritual!

When you finally reach heaven, the place of total spirituality, you would be far removed from where you are commanded to be a witness. Your total dedication to be a truly spiritual witness for Jesus, by being sick, would put you in disobedience to the command to be a witness to all persons on the earth.

If you still believe that it is God's will for you to be sick, why doesn't heaven, the ultimate place of pure spirituality, have sickness? The truth is, Satan is eager to deceive people into believing that God wants them to be sick so that they will be removed from the place where they are to be a mighty witness for Jesus.

How can it be carnal to need money and health in order to proclaim the wondrous works of God? *If health is not spiritual and wealth is not spiritual, I wonder why heaven pulsates with the fullest purity of both?* I believe those who think God wants them to be sick and poor have been deceived. Jesus prayed in Matthew 6:10 that God's will would be done in earth as it is in heaven. This means that God's will in heaven is His will in earth.

Hell is the place of poverty, pain and sickness, not heaven. The Word of God reveals that there is never sickness or need in heaven. God's will is for man to enjoy the pure prosperity that was present when Adam had an intimate relationship with Him. The good gold that God told Adam to dress and keep is street material in heaven. If poverty was spiritual, heaven would be filled with ashes. And if sickness brings glory to God, heaven would be filled with AIDS and every other hideous sickness known to man.

But Jesus welcomed the crowds that followed Him and healed those who needed healing. (Luke 9:10.) And Paul proclaimed that God will meet all our needs according to His glorious riches in Christ Jesus. (Phil. 4:19.)

The *desire* to preach the gospel without the *ability* through health and finances will not win the world to Jesus. We must have divine resources through Christ Jesus to reach all the world with the message of salvation.

Satan's Attack Was Against God's Prosperity Plan

Satan's first attack of deception on man was directed toward God's Plan of Flowing Wealth, His prosperity plan for man. He said, "Yea, hath God said, Ye shall not eat of *every* tree of the garden?" He suggested that God was holding back some possession from Adam and Eve. Satan attacked the exactness of God's Word and His economic plan for man.

Eve held to the Word by repeating that God actually said for them to freely enjoy all the trees *except* the one forbidden tree of the knowledge of good and evil. She said, "We will die if we eat the forbidden tree!"

Satan tempted Eve with the one material possession she did not already own. She had the entire garden available to her, but Satan attacked her pure position of prosperity by telling her there was something more to life than believing the Word of God. Satan said, "You won't die by going against God. God knows your eyes will be opened and you will be like God, knowing good and evil." (Gen. 3:1-7 AMP.)

When the woman saw that the fruit of the tree was good for food and pleasing to the eye, she rationalized that it would make her wise. Then, focusing on self instead of God, she rebelled against Him. She ate the fruit, gave it to her husband, who also ate, and their eyes were opened to the knowledge of good and evil. Immediately they knew they had done an evil thing by disobeying the instructions God had given them concerning the tree.

Satan tricked man over an economic principle. He deceived man into thinking there is more prosperity and material reward apart from God's plan. Satan convinced man to think that disobeying God pays more than obeying Him. Satan always wants man to think that God is not the author of prosperity; Satan wants man to believe God's Plan of Flowing Wealth is inferior to other plans of prosperity.

Satan's deception caused Adam to lose his fellowship with God and his position as ruler over the garden God had given to prosper him.

Man Fell When He Believed Satan's Lie Against God's Prosperity

Since sin, poverty and sickness came into the life of man by Satan's attack against God's prosperity, we should look closely at the same attack on God's plan for prosperity today. Adam did not fall because he was too healthy or because he was too prosperous. Adam fell because he didn't trust the Word of God and believed Satan's lie that there was more gain apart from God than through believing exactly what God had said. God has a Plan of Flowing Wealth for man in the Bible, but man continues to fall whenever he does not believe the exact Word of God.

Man was to work the earth and take care of it. God told man to "rule over" the earth and gave him authority to be in charge of taking care of the land. (Gen.3:15.) Man was expected to be fruitful, multiply, replenish and subdue the earth. He was to have dominion and enjoy the plentifulness of God's riches. But Satan continues to deceive man, either by tempting him to believe there is more to gain than God's best by disobeying Him, or by believing that God is a hard, uncaring God who wants man to learn spiritual lessons through suffering.

Departure From Believing God's Word Brings About the Loss of God's Prosperity

Failure to believe that God is the provider of all good things brought about curses on Adam's life and family. Doubt in God's promises is an act of disobedience and stops the flow of God's provision to man.

Failure to seek an intimate relationship with God brings poverty in all areas of our lives. Departure from faith in God's Word results in a loss of wealth, health, protection, holiness, spirituality, victory and fellowship between God and mankind.

Doubting God's desire to bless His children is a sin against Him, because it is unbelief in the integrity of His Word. This brings curses instead of blessings as a result of a separation from the Father. Psalm 95:10 says, **"Forty years long I was grieved with this generation, and said, It is a people that do err in their heart, and they have not known my ways."** We *grieve* God when we do not know His ways and allow unbelief to fill our hearts.

Believing the Exactness of God's Word Brings Back God's Plan of Flowing Wealth

Poverty came to man when he stopped believing exactly what God had said. Diligent faith in God and believing in the purity of His promises bring the plan of prosperity back to man. Diligence to believe in the exactness of God's Word brings prosperity in all areas of man's life.

When individuals trust God, they can expect spiritual, physical, material, mental, and marital blessings.

Determination to believe that God desires to provide for His children brings the blessings back. When God's people are prospering it glorifies Him.

Repentance Is Required to Reverse the Poverty Curse

To cancel sin and its curse we must repent from any specific sins we are aware of. When we know we have sinned against God's Word by not believing and doing what His Word says, we must repent in order for our sin to be cancelled. When we repent God cancels our sin, which puts us in a position to be blessed. Christians need to believe what the Word of God says to believe in order to reverse the curse of poverty in their lives.

If you have not repented for doubting God's desire to prosper you, the curse of poverty cannot be reversed. Unbelief in what God says in His Word concerning His plan to prosper you is sin, which must be repented of, or the curse of lack remains. When you acknowledge to God that you believe He desires for you to prosper and be in good health, you release His blessings into your life.

Unbelief in Prosperity Is Sin

Scripture shows that unbelief in God's ability and desire to care for His children is sin. God was *grieved* when the children of Israel would not accept His Plan of Flowing Wealth by going into Canaan. He had taken them to the best land, where the greatest resources of the world were located. They had cried out to Him for deliverance from Egyptian bondage, but when He wanted them to go into the land which flowed with His best, they would not go in because of their unbelief.

Why was God displeased with the children of Israel? He was displeased with their unbelief. They believed in God (like you have believed in God). They believed God

24

was the "I AM to all generations." They believed He was the God of their fathers, Abraham, Isaac and Jacob.

They believed Him enough to call on Him for deliverance and to follow Him out of captivity.

They believed Him enough to follow Him to and through the Red Sea.

They believed Him enough to come to the edge of the land that flowed with the best—"the exceedingly good land, flowing with milk and honey."

They believed Him enough to send the twelve leaders to spy out the good land.

They believed in Him enough to repent and praise Him at times.

They believed Him enough to come all the way to the edge of the best.

Consider how greatly they had believed in order to follow Him this far, this long. Why does God say He was "grieved with them and their evil heart of unbelief?" What "evil unbelief" was He grieving over? *They didn't believe He would follow through with His promise to give them His best— the land of flowing wealth.*

Unbelief in God's great Plan of Flowing Wealth for His children is evil and sinful. The children of Israel had committed the *sin of unbelief* in His plan to prosper them.

God's prosperity plan flows with the best this world has to offer. God spoke through Paul in Hebrews 3:6-4:2 and plainly revealed that He was grieved with the children of Israel for the hardness of their hearts against possessing God's best. They would not believe in God's promise of prosperity for them.

Just as Adam's rejection of God's Plan of Flowing Wealth separated him from God's blessings, so were the children of Israel separated from God's blessings because they rejected His promise. They did not believe in His great prosperity plan for their lives. God was grieved by their lack of faith in His Word to them.

To refuse to receive God's Plan of Flowing Wealth is to reject the fellowship of God and the provision that results from an intimate relationship of trusting Him to perform His promises. Rejection of His plan of prosperity is rejection of His Word. When we reject His Plan of Flowing Wealth, we deny Him the opportunity to receive glory for being the God who provides for His children.

What Satan perpetuates is the very opposite of God at all times. Satan is the originator of poverty. To accept anything less than the best of that which flows from God is to accept a part of Satan's plan in your life.

God always offers the very best. He offers all that is good, exceeding abundantly above all that we ask or think. (Eph.3:20.) To accept less than God's blessing is to accept Satan's deception. He is against God's plan to bless you. God's best is what Jesus paid dearly for you to have.

For ye know the grace of our Lord Jesus Christ, that, though he was rich, yet for your sakes he became poor, that ye through his poverty might be rich.

2 Corinthians 8:9

Rich Eden Was God's Plan for Man

Living in the rich garden of Eden was not man's plan for himself; Eden was God's plan for man. Man was to rule over the rich garden of plenty. He was to multiply, increase, subdue, keep, have dominion over it and enjoy all of God's good creation. This was God's original plan for man. He has never changed His plan of plenty for man, and He never will! That's right! He never will! God changes not! God's plan includes forgiveness, health, wealth, protection, dominion and eternal life.

When the children of Israel were under Egyptian bondage, they cried only for deliverance. But God

remembered His covenant with Abraham, in which He
promised to bless Abraham's children and make them a
great nation. So God told Moses to tell the children of Israel
that He had heard their cry for help, and He was going to
do much more than deliver them.

God said to Moses, "Tell them I will lead them to a good
and a large land, unto a land *flowing* with milk and honey
(the best of all things). And with My help, by trusting in
Me, they will be well able to take the land, possess the land
and enjoy the flow of the best in the exceeding good and
fruit-bearing land, which has grape clusters so large it takes
two men to carry them." (Ex. 3:7,8,16,17; Num. 13-14.)

We can see the land that flowed with the best was not
man's plan for man but God's plan for His people, who had
cried only for deliverance. God always remembers *all* of His
covenant, not just part of it, and He continually points man
to the fullness of prosperity.

God says through Paul in Hebrews 4:1, **Let us therefore
fear, lest, a promise being left *us* of entering into his rest,
any of you should seem to come short of it.** God's "rest" is
in the promise of His provision, just as the children of Israel
could have "rested" in the promise He had given them to
inherit Canaan. God had delivered them from Egypt and
tried to get them into the land which flowed with vast
riches, but only Joshua and Caleb believed.

God's promises are for *anyone* who will believe the
fullness of His plan to bless us through Jesus Christ. To
receive His promise, we must be full of faith like Joshua and
Caleb were when they saw the land that God had promised
them. Let us not come short of possessing the prosperity He
has for us. Then we will not displease Him the way the
children of Israel did when they did not believe in His
promise.

To fear and respect God is godly. We are to heed and obey
His Word. We are to know His Word and respectfully

respond to His promises in order to please Him. We are to believe in His Plan of Flowing Wealth. He doesn't want us in the land of "spurt and jerk" blessings. God's prosperity plan for man is an abundant *flow* of blessings. To accept anything less is to accept a contamination of His Word, a contamination coming from Satan, who inspires an evil heart of unbelief. We are to believe in God's prosperity for us.

A Righteous Father Wants the Best for His Children

How can we know that God wants to give us His best? **He that spared not his own Son, but delivered him up for us all, how shall he not with him also freely give us all things?** (Rom. 8:32).

God gave us His best when He gave His Son, Jesus Christ, to die for our salvation. John 3:17 says that God sent His Son that "the world through him might be *saved*." The Greek word for *saved* is *sozo*, which means "to save, deliver or protect: heal, preserve, save (self), do well, be (make) whole." Jesus came that we might be *saved*. In Jesus we see God's grace toward us.

God is righteous and He is Father God, not just God. He is the Almighty Father God who wants His children to receive the blessings He has for them, blessings He paid dearly for them to have. His best is ours because Christ exchanged our poverty for His riches. He took our sin and gave to us His righteousness, that we might inherit the promises of God.

God looks at unbelief in His Plan for Flowing Wealth as "an evil heart of unbelief," a heart that rejects the work of Jesus on the cross. But when we believe in all Jesus did for us in His death and resurrection, we can clearly see that God desires for us to receive His full blessings. So let's find out how to obtain the great wealth which He promised us in His covenant.

2

The Principles of Gaining and Giving

For everyone who has will be given more, and he will have an abundance. Whoever does not have, even what he has will be taken from him.
Matthew 25:29 NIV

Contained within God's Plan for Flowing Wealth are principles for amassing great wealth and distributing it—these are the Principles of Gaining and Giving. They are taught by Jesus in Matthew 25:14-46 and Luke 19:11-26. In this parable about the kingdom of God, Jesus gives the example of the three servants who were entrusted with the master's money, while the master went to a far country to be appointed king. Two of the servants traded with their money and doubled what they were given. The third servant hid the money, fearing that the master would be angry if he was not able to return what was given to him.

When the master returned, he praised the two servants who had traded and gained with their money. He put them both in charge of more wealth, because he knew that they could be trusted to increase what he owned. But the servant who did not use and increase his money was called "wicked" and "lazy." What he was given was taken away and given to the servant who knew how to trade and gain more for the master's use.

In these few verses, Jesus expounds in detail how the master (our Master is God) expected his servants to continually trade, gather and keep (manage) great wealth in order to give it back for the master's use. Jesus said this was like the kingdom of God, illustrating that faithful servants work to gain in order to give more back to the Master than was given to them.

God's Formula for Great Wealth

If the natural principles taught in these verses of Matthew and Luke are followed, God's people can expect an abundance they never dreamed possible. At the same time, they will never diminish the wealth as long as the formula for gaining and giving is obeyed. These are divine principles of prosperity.

Understanding these principles should be viewed with reverence and respectful fear, as Paul spoke of in Hebrews 4:1, **Let us therefore fear, lest, a promise being left us of entering into his rest** [God's best]**, any of you should seem** [fail] **to come short of it.** Paul was referring to the children of Israel, who fell short of God's rest (financial flow, or financial independence) when they refused to enter the land that flowed with milk and honey. He was encouraging New Testament believers not to fall short of receiving God's promises.

In verse 14 of Matthew 25, Jesus says, "The kingdom of heaven is as this," then He tells how the kingdom is to operate in the earth while He goes to heaven and prepares for His return as King, described in verses 31-46. He expects us to work with what we are given and gain in order to give back the prosperity for His use. We are not to be as the wicked, lazy servant, who didn't know his master's heart or understand his instructions.

As you study these verses that define the accumulation and distribution of wealth, you will see that the exact same formula of gaining and giving is illustrated throughout the Bible by Abraham, Isaac, Jacob, Joseph and others. Many biblical examples are given of faithful men and women who used the Principles of Gaining and Giving to accumulate and distribute incredible wealth.

The biblical examples also show how God was pleased by their work. We are told all through the Word of God to follow the faith actions and beliefs of Abraham, whom we call the Father of Faith. Abraham applied the Principles of Gaining and Giving, and he was careful to give God the glory for his wealth. In Genesis 14:23 we see that Abraham wanted the king of Sodom to know that God made him rich, not man! God was well pleased with Abraham's belief.

King David, a man after God's own heart, accumulated and distributed great wealth. David came from poverty and obscurity to great wealth and prominence using the gaining and giving formula. He personally gave over one billion dollars to build the temple of God in Jerusalem.

Did Wealth Cause King David to Sin?

Some Christians believe that wealth caused David to sin. This is not God's thought on David. Neither wealth nor women caused David to sin. The sin of spiritual superiority caused David to sin. His insensitivity to others, his harsh judgment of others and his intolerance of "no sin in others!" caused his fall. David reached the place that he wanted to destroy all the wicked, without exception. He reached the place of "no mercy!" and "condemning judgment." (Ps. 101:7,8.)

This is the same position many people in all socioeconomic positions have taken (including some believers) who are still in poverty. Because of his condemning attitude, David ended up committing every sin he would not tolerate in others.

In God's eyes, riches did not ruin King David. God said to David, after his great sin against his soldier Uriah (2 Sam. 11), **"I anointed thee king over Israel, and I delivered thee out of the hand of Saul; and I gave thee thy master's**

house, [the castle of the king], and thy master's wives into thy bosom, and gave thee the house of Israel and of Judah; *and if that had been too little, I would moreover have given unto thee such and such things.* **Wherefore hast thou despised the commandment of the Lord, to do evil in his sight?** (2 Sam. 12:7-9).

God did not associate David's sin with great wealth. God certainly did not imply that riches caused David to sin. God's Word to David was, "If all of these things I have given you was too little, I would have given you much, much more!"

It is interesting to see how much more positive God is about great wealth than we "spiritual" people are. God, who is totally spiritual, seems to value it preciously. *All* the wealth of the earth was at one time under His control in heaven and in earth. He committed the care of His wealth in the earth to Adam, and the family of man was to look after it just like God had.

But Adam disobeyed and let God's abundance slip out of his hands. Adam was supposed to *dress* and *keep* the wealth of God's world over which he was put in charge. (Gen.2:15.) He was to till, cultivate and fertilize the fields and plants in Eden. Adam was to protect, guard and defend the prosperous garden over which God had put him in charge.

Working, protecting, multiplying and controlling the fruit of your labor is a key to the formula of accumulating great wealth for God. God's first command to us is to be fruitful, multiply, replenish and subdue the earth. We are to accumulate and control earth's great riches for God.

God Controls the World Wealth Through the Obedient Man

As a Christian, you are God's servant, and one of your duties is controlling His wealth in the world. He accumulates and distributes His wealth through His obedient people.

How is God doing where you are concerned? Is He wealthy or broke? If everyone believed the same as you do about the use and control of money, how much money would God have under His control in the earth? Would God be doing well if everyone was operating their finances like you, or is He disadvantaged?

Matthew 25:14-46 tells you fully how God wants you to operate financially in His kingdom on earth. He gave the control of the wealth to Adam, who lost control to Satan. Now He wants to *legally* get the wealth of the world back under His loving control through you, His child. You can accumulate wealth for God's purposes by being obedient to His Principles of Gaining and Giving. You can be the servant whom He puts in charge over much by being a good steward over whatever amount you have now.

The Consequence of Refusing to Possess the Best for God

When the children of Israel refused to go into the great flourishing land that was their promised heritage through Abraham, they were leaving the best of the world's resources in the hands of a people who did not serve or honor God. They were leaving the world's wealth in the hands of a people who would not give God the tithe from the firstfruits (the first tenth, which is God's). As a result, the best of this earth's resources was in the hands of a people who would not use it for God, worship God with it or because of it. God had no control, benefit, revenue or praise for the best of the earth's resources.

God's people were holding to barren existence in the desert wilderness. They chose a lifestyle which generated complaint instead of praise. Ultimate poverty produces complaint, not praise. Ultimate poverty is filled with pain, distress and "praiselessness." The children of Israel remained in distress because *poverty and the lack of plenty are not God's will!*

A lack of abundance is disobedience to God's Plan of Flowing Wealth for man. God created man to be in charge over the fertile, flourishing, multiplying, extraordinarily special and rich, luxurious existence of Eden. To hold to a skimpy barrenness is to deny God the rich bounty of plenty and praise He deserves for His creation. He gave the earth to the children of men for His glory and for His children to enjoy and flourish in—for His majestic pleasure.

No Money or Praise for God

Do you see how the children of Israel were wrong for not going in to possess the best for God's glory? He received no praise or benefit from these resources when it was in the hands of those who were not living for Him.

The exact same thing happens today when you refuse to accumulate great wealth for God and then distribute it to His glory. The promised land was His will for all His people. Yet, out of three million people only three individuals, Moses, Joshua and Caleb, would discipline themselves to believe in God's Plan for Flowing Wealth in the promised land.

God wants you to do what the unbelieving would not do. He wants you to acquire His superior best from a flourishing earth of great riches for Him now. God wants you to be wealthy for the same reasons He wanted the children of Israel to be in His best land. He wants control of the earth's best for His use through believers, and He wants praise from His blessed children who have obediently dressed and kept the riches of the earth just like He wanted Adam to do.

Jesus tells you how God originally intended for you to prosper for Him in Matthew 25:14-46. God's Principles of

Gaining and Giving are clearly explained in these verses, and these same principles are revealed throughout the Bible. These principles of financial abundance have been right in your New Testament for nearly two thousand years!

Now let's go into detail and understand these principles by studying the exactness of what Jesus said. Praise God for revealing truth from His Word to keep us in His perfect will!

Jesus Taught Gaining and Giving Together

Jesus taught the importance of sequential gaining and giving in His sermon on the Mount of Olives through the parable of the servants, who gained by trading, and through the illustration of the righteous and the unrighteous, who were separated like sheep from goats, according to whether or not they ministered to the needs of Jesus.

In Matthew 25:14-30, Jesus taught the principle of gaining by trading, managing, and accepted no excuses for not gaining abundantly in the marketplaces of life. In Matthew 25:31-46, Jesus taught the principle of giving to Him, based on His followers taking care of the needs of those in that same marketplace of life. He did not accept any excuses for not supplying these needs. We will not be excused from our responsibility to give to Him by saying, "But Lord, I didn't have the money to meet those needs."

We should be *warned* that we too could hear the response of, "You wicked and lazy servant! If you didn't want to work to *gain* money, you should have at least *saved* your money and used the interest to give back to Me for ministry."

Jesus taught gaining and giving in the same sermon, to the same audience. These are the *two major principles of financial abundance* that were taught by Jesus as one complete message. Neither the gaining principle nor the giving principle was neglected, so God's Plan of Flowing Wealth would be balanced and operate in the lives of all believers who are obedient to apply it.

Success Requires Balance

God's plan for all of His children to receive the full abundance of wealth is dependent upon the balance of the gaining and giving principles. You cannot have great financial success and please God without an equal application of both.

Gaining without giving is imbalanced and will not produce the lasting abundance God has planned for all of His children to have. Giving without a plan to gain will not give you the abundance God intends for you either. These principles of God require balance of receiving wealth and distributing wealth in order to continue expressing the abundance of God's plan. Here are some other examples of balance in the Word of God:

- Faith is balanced with works, for faith without works is dead. (James 2:17.)

- Spiritual gifts are balanced with love. (1 Cor.13:2.)

- Your being forgiven is balanced by your forgiveness of others. (Matt. 6:12.)

- Answered prayer is balanced with belief. (Matt. 21:22.)

- Ministry is balanced with a life of prayer. (John 14:12-14.)

Jesus did not let the crowds keep Him from prayer, but He did not let prayer keep Him from the crowds. He balanced what He received from God in prayer by giving to others. He prayed early in the morning and sometimes all night. Jesus had temporal seasons of seeking God, but He ministered throughout the day in the marketplaces of humanity.

The purpose of Jesus' prayers was for ministry and not for cloistered seclusion. The reason He prayed early in the day was to prepare for His ministry to the needs of humanity. Jesus gave to mankind all the good things of God. Consistent prayer without purposeful ministry is imbalanced. Consistent ministry without consistent prayer is imbalanced.

All of God's principles have balance, including the financial Principles of Gaining and Giving which Jesus taught for us to use in the earth.

You Must Have Balance by Both Gaining and Giving

Purposeful and unlimited *giving must be balanced* with the implementation of purposeful and unlimited gain. You should have plans of consistent gain so that you will be able to consistently give. Giving without gaining and without a plan to regain more to give is death in the financial arena of your life.

Purposeful and unlimited *gain must be balanced* with the implementation of purposeful and unlimited giving. Ruin is imminent when giving does not flow from your life with the same intensity you have for gaining. Expecting gain without the fervent zeal to give into God's kingdom is an imbalance that will insure consistent loss of God's Plan for Flowing Wealth for you.

Our purpose for giving and gaining, gaining and giving, should be from our desire to do things exactly God's way. When we do things God's way, we are abundantly equipped to fulfill His will in the earth. It is His will to be in control of the accumulation and distribution of our finances. We are to give, in the name of Jesus, to the legitimate needs listed in Matthew 25:31-46 of all individuals we encounter with these needs. As these verses plainly state, we are to do this without excuse.

As servants of God who are to be suppliers in His name and witnesses of His great love, we must draw from His abundant resources to minister to others His way. His perfect way is through abundant gaining by trading and then through abundant giving.

If you have desired to be a giver but have not had plans of gaining in the marketplaces of life, you are not equipped to give consistently to the needs of people in the way Jesus required in Matthew 25:34-40. If you have not been financially able to consistently give with the abundant intensity Jesus points out in this gaining and giving teaching, then you probably are not aware of the importance of gaining.

Gaining in order to give is a divine principle of balance which is necessary for the flow of God's abundant financial provision, which He desires His sons and daughters to distribute through godly stewardship. It is an act of disobedience not to give abundantly, but it is also an act of disobedience not to gain abundantly. God has given each of His servants unique and specific ways to gain by trading in the daily marketplaces of life.

Jesus Gained by Trading

We know that Jesus did not use miracles to meet the needs of others until after He was thirty years old. Up to the time of His full-time ministry, Jesus was well-known as the carpenter from Nazareth, and His skill was tied to His identity in the marketplaces of Israel. Through His experience as a carpenter in Nazareth, Jesus knew firsthand that the Principles of Gaining and Giving work.

It seems obvious that, as a carpenter, Jesus worked the Principle of Gaining through His work and then gave to the needs of others. He most likely gave to the support of His mother through the trading and gaining of His carpentry skills.

It appeared that Joseph was no longer alive when, from the cross, Jesus asked John to take care of His mother after His departure. Being the oldest brother, Jesus had probably taken responsibility for His mother's needs once Joseph was gone. This resposibility was important enough to Jesus that He mentioned it in His last moments on the cross.

It is also reasonable to assume that Jesus practiced *all* that He preached—and He certainly taught that all should gain by trading. We know Jesus defined giving as a godly principle in Matthew 25:31-46, because He knew it would be a temptation for us not to give.

As Jesus was *tempted* in all the ways we are tempted, He must have been tempted not to gain by trading, to give everything away, and never charge for His services. He above all others had to practice *balance* by faith, regardless of imbalanced feelings. As we walk in obedience to His teachings, we are an example even in the area of finances.

But He also demonstrated clearly how we can become an instrument of His grace to others by trusting Him and using the skills He has given us to work and expect blessing on the return of our labor. The financial blessing could then be used to bring the Gospel to and meet the needs of others.

The purpose of the Principles of Gaining and Giving is to successfully finance the ministry of God's kingdom to the world. If these principles are neglected by God's children, then His divine will, which is to reach maximum provision to supply the needs of humanity in the name of Jesus, cannot be fulfilled.

3

Matthew's Account of Gaining by Trading

Matthew 25:14-30 teaches *abundant Gaining by Trading* as a kingdom of heaven principle of increasing wealth for ministry on earth. Matthew 25:31-46 teaches *abundant giving to the needs of others* as a kingdom of heaven principle for ministering as unto Jesus.

In this chapter, we're going to examine the Principle of Gaining by Trading. Let's begin with verse 14 of Matthew, chapter 25:

> For *the kingdom of heaven* is as a man travelling into a far country, *who* called his own servants, and delivered unto them his goods.
>
> And unto one he gave five talents, to another two, and to another one; to every man according to his several ability; and straightway took his journey.
>
> Then he that had received the five talents went and traded with the same, and made *them* other five talents.
>
> And likewise he that *had received* two, he also gained other two.
>
> But he that had received one went and digged in the earth, and hid his lord's money.
>
> After a long time the lord of those servants cometh, and reckoneth with them.
>
> And so he that had received five talents came and brought other five talents, saying, Lord, thou deliveredst unto me five talents: behold, I *have gained* beside them five talents more.

His lord said unto him, Well done, *thou* good and faithful servant: thou hast been faithful over a few things, I will make thee ruler over many things: enter thou into the joy of thy lord.

He also that had received two talents came and said, Lord, thou deliveredst unto me two talents: behold, I have gained two other talents beside them.

His lord said unto him, Well done, good and faithful servant; thou hast been faithful over a few things, I will make thee ruler over many things: enter thou into the joy of thy lord.

Then he which had received the one talent came and said, Lord, I knew thee that thou art an hard man, reaping where thou hast not sown, and gathering where thou hast not strawed:

And I was afraid, and went and hid thy talent in the earth: lo, *there* thou hast *that* is thine.

His lord answered and said unto him, *Thou* wicked and slothful servant, thou knewest that I reap where I sowed not, and gather where I have not strawed:

Thou oughtest therefore to have put my money to the exchangers, and *then* at my coming I should have received mine own with *usury*.

Take therefore the talent from him, and give it unto him which hath ten talents.

For unto every one that hath shall be given, and he shall have abundance: but from him that hath not shall be taken away even that which he hath.

And cast ye the unprofitable servant into outer darkness: there shall be weeping and gnashing of teeth.

Matthew 24:14-30

Jesus said that the kingdom of heaven operates as a man who went to a far country. This symbolizes Jesus going to heaven after His resurrection. The same story is told in Luke 19:11-26, where the nobleman left *money* with his servants while he went away to be appointed king. He told the servants, "Occupy till I come." This has been translated in the *New International Version* as **Put this money to work until I come back.** *The Amplified Bible* translated this as, **Buy** *and* **sell with these while I go** *and* **return.**

The master entrusted his property and wealth with his own servants just as God entrusted Adam and Eve with the responsibility of Eden and Jesus has entrusted us with abilities to trade and gain. This parable illustrates exactly what the Lord intends for His children whom He places over His good earth.

His commandment to dress, keep, *multiply,* subdue, and enjoy all the superior, plush, abundance He has created has not changed. Jesus won back our inheritance that Adam lost when He redeemed us from the curse of the law through His death and made us joint-heirs with Him through His resurrection and grace. The superior, plush abundance is now in our hands.

To every servant, the master gave talents according to his individual ability. This was a measurement of value in silver and gold, or material wealth, recognized as exchange for goods and services. Each talent was worth more than one million dollars of gold or $21,000 of silver by today's standard. So you see, Jesus used large amounts of money in illustrating His teachings on gaining by trading.

Jesus Spoke of Great Amounts of Money in His Teaching Illustrations

Jesus is clearly speaking of the stewardship of money. Verse 27 states that the wicked servant who hid the talent should have placed the master's *money* with the exchangers (bankers) so it could have earned usury (interest).

Those who were faithful over the wealth that had been entrusted to them were put over many cities. Being over ten cities is a large amount of material wealth to be over.

A talent represented a large amount of gold or silver. The servants listed received between two to ten million dollars to trade and gain with. Remember, Adam was put over good gold in the garden of Eden, and he was instructed to work and take care of it (dress and keep it). (Gen. 1:28; 2:11-13.) Likewise, *everyone today* is given personal ability to gain by trading. You have been given unique abilities to trade in the marketplace by which you can gain wealth for the Master's use.

The servant who received the five talents *traded* with the same. He went to the *marketplaces* of life and doubled what he had been given by trading with others. *The New International Version* of the Bible says, "This man **went at once and put his *money* to *work** and gained." This means the man who was given five talents *made* over ten million dollars.

Eventually the master returned and called the servants to find out *how much every man had gained by trading.* (Luke 19:15.) The servants who had gained acknowledged that they understood they were supposed to *increase* the *money.* They had obeyed the lord of the kingdom and realized it was the *lord's money.* These servants were praised and given even more.

When God checked with Adam to see how he had gained in the garden, what did Adam report? Adam had given it all to the deceiver. Adam lost all that he was given through his disobedience of not believing God.

What would your report be today if Jesus checked to see how well you were doing in gaining wealth for His use in the kingdom of heaven? Perhaps you would defend yourself with, "I didn't know I was supposed to gain with Your money." But through this teaching from Jesus, we can see how to become the givers we have wanted to be and He requires us to be. We can also understand how to enjoy the abundance our righteous Father desires His obedient children to enjoy with Him. **Come and share your master's happiness!** (Matt. 25:23 NIV).

It Is Important to Gain for the Kingdom

How can you begin? Buying a bargain at one garage sale and selling it at another garage sale for more is an obvious way in the simplest form. Selling what you have is obedience to the divine principle of trading and gaining.

If all we have is a small amount of money, we are to seek the Lord in finding a way to use it to trade our ability in the market at a profitable gain. We are not to hide our finances in fear of losing it, like the servant who dug a whole in the earth.

The servant with one talent did not lose or decrease the money. But because he did nothing at all with the talent, the master called him "wicked and lazy." This man didn't give or gain. He did nothing and lost even what he had. He violated both Principles of Gaining and Giving. Because of fear, he didn't do either.

Not only does this man lose all his money, the story implies he lost his life prematurely. Matthew 25:30 says the worthless servant was thrown into darkness, where there was weeping and gnashing of teeth—a place of not knowing and being excluded from what God was doing in the earth. The account in Luke 19 infers he was among the enemies who were to be killed in front of the king.

This passage of Scripture is talking about the stewardship or business management of money. It has been covered up by traditional teaching that, "It's spiritual to be poor and carnal to be wealthy! Sell *all* you have and give to the poor and never sell again." This puts you in the same category of the poor to whom you just gave!

If every person on earth adopted this philosophy of false spirituality, selling *all* they had, giving to the poor and never planning to sell again, the whole world would be impoverished. Who would give to the poor then? You can't give to the poor consistently, or more than one time, if you sell all you have and give to the poor without the resources to gain wealth again.

Jesus didn't even ask the rich young ruler to sell all until he showed dissatisfaction in doing all the law. (Luke 18:22.) It appears that he was not giving to God. Jesus said that those who *trusted* in riches could not enter the kingdom. (Mark 10:24.)

In the same account recorded in Matthew 19:16-29, Peter asked Jesus what he and the other apostles would receive for entrusting all to Jesus and following Him. Jesus said that the twelve would sit on thrones in the world to come, but in this life they would receive one hundred times more of *whatever* they had entrusted to Him. Jesus also said that this was a promise to *everyone* who committed all to Him. (v. 29.)

Traditionally, we have also been taught not to have money like the apostles had no money—especially if we are ministers. This teaching was based on scriptures where Jesus told His disciples to take no money with them when they ministered. But Jesus was not telling them they should not have wealth.

He was saying not to take money in "their *purses*. . . for the servant (full-time minister) is worthy of his *hire* (pay for spiritual duties performed)." Jesus told this to the twelve (Matt. 10:5-10) and to the seventy (Luke 10:1-7). He was telling them not to take finances from home when they travelled to minister, but to expect *good pay* where they preached the Gospel (and part of the Good News is how to gain and give).

Adam obeyed Satan because he thought he would receive more than he already had through the promises of God. But instead He gave up God's Plan for Flowing

Wealth when he believed the lie that Satan's plan would bring him a greater reward. He gave up God's wealth, which he had been put over to *increase*, keep (manage) and enjoy.

When we refuse to be good stewards over all that God has given us and refuse to increase what has been entrusted to us with the work of our hands, we do what Adam did. We give up the Lord's garden of flowing wealth with which He commanded us to be fruitful, *multiply* and subdue its vast resources. We give up the abundance that the Lord told us to tend, guard and keep.

The servants in this story who gained with their business abilities knew the character of their lord. They knew their master would be pleased with the increase they had gained through trading. Our Lord wants to be worshipped with the firstfruits of our increase. He has not asked us to worship Him with the firstfruits of the decrease, but with the firstfruits of the increase (the gain).

The master said in verse 21, "Well done good [not bad] and faithful servant: you have been faithful over a few things, I will make you ruler over many things." The statement, "You have been faithful over," was the lord's comment, with determination to reward his profit-making servant for the great increase of money. He neither reprimanded the servant for greed, nor did he accuse the servant of unfaithfulness for not selling all and giving *everything* to the poor. The master also didn't tell the servant that he should have put *everything* he had in ministry.

This servant was able to give the increase to his lord because he used what he was given to work with and refused to lose it through idleness. The lord rewarded this faithful servant by giving him greater wealth to rule over and inviting him to enter into his joy. Joy comes from fulfilling the expectations of the Lord by increasing in wealth through gaining by trading, according to His Plan of Flowing Wealth.

The lord said, "I" (the lord) "will make you *master over many things* because you have been faithful to be master over a few things." Our Lord will make us master over many things when we are faithful to *increase* what we are given to start with. Then He says, "I will make you ruler over many things."

When you increase what you have been given with *consistency* and *permanence,* this shows that you rule over things and things do not rule you. If you are consistently and permanently in need, then the things you need are ruling over you. You are at the mercy of whatever it is you need.

When you do not cause increase by trading and selling your goods and services in the earth, things are ruling you. As a servant of God's kingdom, you have been given a *command to rule* over what you have. You can do this with a plan and determination to increase by charging well for your goods and services. A failure to do so is to allow things to rule you.

To increase honestly, in obedience to Jesus' emphasis on gaining by trading, is to prove you will rule over the talents entrusted to you. To not increase is to "be ruled over." The Lord of the kingdom is displeased with disobedience to a kingdom principle of success for both His kingdom and you.

If you decrease, you will contribute to the loss and failure of the church's ability to meet the needs of people. When you, through good stewardship and business management, rule over your business skills with a plan and determination to increase, you insure the gain and success of God's kingdom. Be counted among those who are faithful over the talents (money) entrusted to you and be prepared to receive more from Him, to faithfully distribute and manage His wealth over even larger areas.

It is important to notice that the servants gained more talents (money) through their own ability to manage what was given to them. The lord did not bless them with more money. They gained more money through trading. The blessing from the lord came after the servants had been faithful to follow the lord's instructions and double what they were originally given.

When we refuse to gain, we are in disobedience to God. When we continue to need more and survive in a bare existence, we are not receiving the blessings the Lord has in mind for us. Our lives are not glorifying Him with evidence that He is a God who loves and provides for His children. If we are begging bread, we are not receiving His promises.

His mercy maintains us when our blindness to His abundant, unlimited, benevolent, everflowing blessings keep us in disobedience. But He wants us to live in the land that *flows* with milk and honey. He has an abundant, unhindered flow of blessings to bestow on us that will bring glory to Him. Our key to flowing blessings is to obediently increase and manage the abilities He gives us.

Our faithfulness to increase for Him with what we have (like the faithful servants did) insures His trusting us to be ruler over many things. Being entrusted by God to "rule over many things" depends on how well we *gain* by trading what we now have.

"Doubling Your Money" With Apples and Hubcaps

If you have one apple, all you need is another apple to double what you have to be an obedient servant. Your aim to gain by trading, which is the way Jesus said to gain for the kingdom, is to sell the apple you have at a better market price than what you bought it for. Your aim for God is to be wise in *buying* and wise in *selling*. Be wise to buy low and sell high. The key to ruling over much is to always sell what you have for *gain* and keep your *expenses lower* than your income.

If, for example, you are in the car business and you wish you had many cars and a nice building to sell them in, then you must start where you are with the determination to sell what you have at an increase. If you only have enough to buy two hubcaps to sell now, find a place to buy them cheaply. Then find a market that will pay you much more than your purchase price. Let this be your lifestyle as a child of the King. To consistently gain by trading is to obey the first principle of God's Plan for Flowing Wealth. Operating the Principle of Gaining by Trading is obeying God and a key to your success.

Your motivation for determining to rule over your money should be so that the Lord can direct you how to use the increase while you rule over it for Him. This is what Adam should have done, but he was negligent and did not rule over the garden he was given.

We are to rule over and to increase our money for God without exception. *This is a kingdom principle of success.* In verse 26 of Matthew 25, the lord answered the servant who did not trade and gain with the one talent he was given, "You wicked and slothful servant." The servant had admitted that he knew how his lord operated, so he was willfully disobedient to his instructions. His excuse was that he feared what would happen if he didn't gain, so he chose to do nothing with the talent (at least one million dollars).

The lord said he was slothful, which means tardy, indolent and irksome! The servant didn't follow the master's example to earn an increase with the talent, and the lord was very displeased with his failure. He called him negligent for not making a great amount of money for the kingdom by using the Principle of Gaining by Trading.

Likewise, there is no acceptable excuse for a Christian to not gain by trading and increase wealth for the kingdom of God while on the earth.

The Increase of People and Money for the Kingdom Depends on You

We must obey God's principles in all areas of life for His kingdom to fully operate on earth. We are to testify of God's goodness to all mankind in order to increase the number of believers who will inherit the kingdom of God. Growth of the church depends on our obedience as His servants to win men, women and children to Jesus, the Lord and Savior.

The *financial increase* of the kingdom also depends upon our obedience as God's servants to apply the financial Principle of Gaining by Trading with what we have and giving in obedience to God from the firstfruits of the increase. The increase of *believers and finances* for God's work depends on obedient servants who will *win* and *gain* as Jesus taught.

Disobedience to win people to Jesus by sharing our testimony and ministering to their needs will not increase the numbers in the kingdom. To not win souls violates a principle that Jesus taught and denies the increase of souls for the kingdom.

Disobedience to the Principle of Gaining by Trading will not increase the finances of the kingdom either. To not increase wealth by trading your goods and services violates a principle Jesus taught and denies financial increase for the kingdom.

Legal Ways to Get God's Money Back

Jesus said, "The kingdom of heaven is as *this*," meaning it works like this in the earth. Jesus showed us a natural application of how to gain financial wealth by trading with our business abilities and how to bring that increase back to the one it originally belonged to. We are to do the same by bringing our increase back to Jesus for His use to meet the needs of others defined in Matthew 25:31-46.

The fullness of kingdom riches is in heaven, so no increase is needed there. But an increase is needed on the earth in order to minister to others. Adam lost God's riches in the earth. The wealth fell from God's people and was left for the hands of the wicked until Jesus fulfilled God's plan of redemption and brought sons and daughters into His kingdom. Now, the *legal way* to get the earth's wealth back is through gain by honest trade.

The greatest way to finance evangelism is through the sale of goods and services. Another way to get the wealth of the world into the kingdom of God is through winning those with whom you trade to Jesus. When a man or woman gives their life to Jesus, they will begin to use their riches for work in the kingdom as well. They now belong to Jesus and so does their wealth. It is legally His after they give themselves to Him.

As you trade with individuals, you have multiple opportunities to win them to Christ with your fair business practices and your uplifting Christian attitude. Consistently pray and expect the Holy Spirit to show you how to win them as you trade with them. It is a positive witness to unbelievers when they see your success in the business field and realize that you give Jesus the glory for the principles of increase you have applied.

Trade your goods and services for gain, either by buying products from others to sell at a higher price elsewhere or by selling your services to them. Increase by trade with them until you win them. Then increase by trade with them after you win them. They will increase from your goods and services and you will increase from theirs. It is a kingdom principle.

Interest Is the Least Accepted Way to Gain

Well then, you should have put my money on deposit with the *bankers*, so that when I returned I would have received it back with *interest*.

Matthew 25:27 NIV

Isn't this interesting? Jesus teaches here that the servant should have deposited his money in a bank where it would have drawn interest, rather than let it sit idle in a hiding place. This illustrates that money should always be working somewhere. Even the banker knows to use money to meet the needs of people and pay interest for the use of the money. But a savings account was the least acceptable way to increase finances.

The most desirable way of increasing finances for God's use is by trading for gain by doubling what you start with. Gaining by bank interest is better than not gaining, but gaining by trading is better than just having your money draw interest.

The talent was taken from the slothful servant who refused to work and was given to the one who had made the greatest increase. It almost seems unfair, but the master is the one who said, "Take it and give it to the one who has ten talents." Jesus wanted us to know this story for a reason. More was given to the man who had made the *most*. More was given to the servant who *knew* how to increase for the master's use.

All was taken from the unrepentant, disobedient servant who only made excuses. Unrepentant sin, even in the area of failure to increase finances for the kingdom, brings the curse of loss, but obedience to this Plan for Flowing Wealth receives great *reward*. Taking the money from the wicked servant who wouldn't use it and giving it to the righteous servant who traded with it is another example of the wealth of the wicked being put into the hands of the righteous.

It's Also a Sin to Cheat Yourself

Financial failure caused by slothfulness and an unwillingness to work is an act of unrighteousness. A slothful person who refuses to gain by trading cheats himself, his family and God's kingdom.

God is not pleased with cheating, even when we cheat ourselves. He rewards the fair and honest with blessing. Unfairness and dishonesty even to yourself remove you from God's reward, bringing a curse instead of a blessing. David was aware of this concept when he wrote this psalm:

> **Blessed is the man who fears the Lord, who finds great delight in his commands.**
>
> **His children will be mighty in the land; the generation of the upright will be blessed.**
>
> *Wealth and riches are in his house*, **and his righteousness endures forever.**
>
> **Psalm 112:1-3 NIV**

The Key to Having Abundance

> **For unto *every one that hath* shall be given, and he shall have abundance: but from him that hath not shall be taken away even that which he hath.**
>
> **Matthew 25:29**

Gaining and keeping wealth, not hiding and losing money, is the key to having abundance. The amazing point of this verse is that *everyone* who has will be given abundantly more, and *whoever* does not have will lose even what he has.

Have you ever known anyone who seems to always be without? They are without throughout life. Yet those who have seem to always have throughout life. This story holds the key to having or never having. To grasp the truth of this verse is to grasp the blessing of abundant supply and avoid financial failure. The keys to "have" or "not to have" are in this verse and hold your future of "being in plenty" or "being in want."

In order to have abundance in your life, you must trade your goods or services for gain and bring your increase to the Lord for His direction. To be in poverty and lack provision you must sit idle, hide what you have been given, fail to increase wealth and return your unused money to the Lord for His direction. He will then direct money from you to the one who knows how to put it to work. Then it will increase.

As you rule over your money by being a good steward (business manager for God) of what you have been given, you will always have more. I don't care how small your beginning is. When you refuse to lose and make it your business to gain by trading with what you now have (using your talent, abilities, crafts, ideas or inventions), you will soon have an abundance to share with others, and you will never be without the things you need.

It is important to understand that you are applying a *divine* principle when you determine to rule over what you have and ask God for a plan to increase by trading for profit in the marketplaces of your life. This is how God can bless you and give you more. This is how God's abundance is distributed to all of His children.

Increase your finances by trading for profit with what you have and never allow decrease to take place for any reason. Increasing, not decreasing, is the key of consistently having enough, which keeps you in the divine position of abundant giving and living!

4
The Principle of Increase Without Loss

God's Plan of Flowing Wealth works throughout the Bible. In fact, Abraham applied the financial principles that Jesus taught two thousand years before Jesus lived. Abraham learned to always increase and never decrease what he had been given to tend, guard and keep. Genesis 13:2 reports that He was very rich in cattle, silver and gold. He had become wealthy in these three areas, which he concentrated on at that particular time. He was rich in other areas later.

Remember, in Matthew 25 the master promised the faithful servant that he would make him to be ruler over many things because he was faithful over a few things. Obviously, the ten cities he was rewarded had many categories of wealth, including livestock, agriculture, trade and commerce. God promises to give more than what we already have when we are faithful to rule over and increase what we are given.

Abraham Always Increased and Refused to Lose

Abraham increased what he was given and refused to take a loss. He was prepared to keep what he had been faithful to increase. He trained and armed 318 elite fighting men in order to protect what he had. They rose up to fight when the armies of many unrighteous kings stole goods from him and his nephew, Lot.

Abraham did not fold his hands and say, "The Lord gives and the Lord takes away. Blessed be the name of the Lord." He did not say, "Where did I miss God?" and then begin to seek God. He knew that he was to be faithful over what had been given to him to guard and protect. He amassed and kept great wealth. He is an example of the divine Principle of Gaining by Trading. (Matt. 25:29.) Abraham kept what he had and gained with it. He refused to lose! When what he had was threatened, he went after what was taken and recovered all and more.

It Is a Spiritual Law to Increase!

God's Word reveals it is His will for you to win and not to lose when you serve Him. An important part of being sucessful is *knowing* it is God's will for you to increase. We know God told Adam to work, multiply, subdue and keep the garden. This was God's command to *mankind*. We also know from the teachings of Jesus (Matt. 25:14-30) that we are to trade with what we are given and gain an increase for Him.

The Principles of Gaining by Trading and Increase Without Loss were active in the life of Abraham. He had great wealth because he *knew* it was God's will for him to increase it and keep it. He was so confident of God's will, he was prepared to fight with his well-trained troops to recover what had been taken from him by the kings who were at war with each other.

It Is a Spiritual Principle to Recover What Is Stolen

When Abraham's goods were stolen by these kings, He planned, organized and fought to recover what his enemies had taken from him. He knew to keep his goods for the purpose of enforcing God's commandment to guard, protect, keep, control and multiply what had been given him for God's kingdom. (Gen. 14:13-17.)

Abraham did not blindly pursue the recovery of his goods either. He devised a *plan* to divide his forces and attack his enemies from more than one direction. He attacked the kings by night and persisted until he defeated them. Abraham was crafty and did not give up until he *repossessed* everything taken from him and his nephew, Lot. (Gen. 14:15,16).

To *recover* what has been stolen by our enemy is a spiritual principle of the kingdom of heaven. To devise a plan of recovery is also a spiritual principle that biblical examples encourage us to follow. To pray and ask God for a successful plan of recovery for every area in which we have lost is a *spiritual* thing to do.

God blessed Job with twice as much in every area in which he lost. David recovered all he lost when he devised a *plan* by seeking God. (1 Sam. 30:18.) He was made king of Israel after he was faithful to recover all he had lost. David's life demonstrated God's Plan of Flowing Wealth for those who seek first the kingdom of heaven.

(I encourage you to write to my ministry address at the back of this book and request my tapes on recovery entitled, "Planning to Recoup in Every Area You Have Lost In," "God Really Blessed Abraham When He Repossessed," and "No Excuse Is Good Enough for Losing." These messages will encourage you to *plan to repossess* what the devil has taken.)

Abraham's Reward for Being Faithful Over What He Had

The example of how the Lord gave Abraham victory in his *planned* recovery is an illustration of the financial principles in Matthew 25, especially how the Lord gives mastery over more when you are faithful over the little you are given. Abraham proved faithful to be over much and God rewarded him by giving him victory over his enemies and restoring all that was taken. (Gen. 14:16.)

Abraham did not need encouragement, monetary wealth or protection, because he increased and never allowed a loss to have victory over him. The Word of the Lord came to him in a vision saying, **Fear not, Abram: I am thy** *shield* [protection], **and thy exceeding great** *reward* (Gen. 15:1).

Abraham had applied the biblical principle of being faithful over the great material wealth of God. He successfully trusted God as he kept and protected what was his. Adam had the opportunity to trust God this same way, but he failed. For us today, God *still rewards* those who are faithful over little with more.

Increase By Being Faithful Over What You Have

When you *prove* to be faithful over what God has given you to dress and keep, regardless of apparent great loss, God applies the divine Principle of Reward because you refused to lose. David proved faithful to recover all and was rewarded with more. Regardless of what appeared to be great loss, David recovered *all*. He was rewarded and entrusted with the wealth of Israel when God appointed him king.

In later years David, who had at one time referred to himself as a poor man (1 Sam. 18:23), gave over a *billion* dollars from his *personal* treasury to build God's first temple of worship in the earth. (1 Chron. 29:1-5.) David was blessed with much because he was dedicated to God and because he applied the Plan of Flowing Wealth for the success of God's kingdom by gaining, maintaining and giving.

To maintain is to be faithful over what we are given. Neither Abraham nor David gave an excuse for their losses. Each of them had a *plan* for *recovery*. If you are not planning to recover in every area in which you have lost, you are not applying God's principles of financial success. You should ask God for a plan and do what David and Abraham did to recoup all and more than they had lost. As I said before, to plan for recovery of all you have lost is a *spiritual* thing to do.

(I will suggest one more tape. I believe this tape will help you with your finances. The title is, "Planning to Profit Is a Spiritual Principle Whether You Feel it is Spiritual or Not.")

Everyone Is Called to Be Faithful Over What They Have

I believe Abraham used the Principle of Gaining by Trading, because Genesis 13:2 says he *became* wealthy in cattle, silver and gold. Chapter 12:5 says he *accumulated* possessions. He was a leader who ruled over these possessions and looked after great numbers of people whom he acquired in Haran. To have wealth in cattle, it seems that he must have known the "cattle business" and used his ability there to maintain his livestock and increase the number.

Nevertheless, you can have your own "gold mine" like Abraham had by developing your business abilities and selling your goods and services for gain. Then rule over the increase like Abraham did for God. Abraham's life is an example of God's will for *everyone* in His kingdom.

Abraham applied the principle of being a faithful steward and reaped the benefits defined in Matthew 25:29, which says, "Everyone who has shall be given more, and he shall have abundance." You are included in this promise. *Everyone is included in God's plan to provide abundantly for the people on earth.* God loves mankind and has enough to provide for everyone. He wants to work through believers to reach unbelievers with the Good News of abundant life through Jesus Christ.

As you apply this principle of being faithful over what God has entrusted to you, more will be given to you in abundance. The Principle of Gaining by Trading that Jesus taught includes you. Verse 15 says that *every* man was given talents to gain by trading according to his abilities. The more skills you develop, the more will be given to you. You are to maintain your financial growth and increase it through the abilities you have.

Then you are to give out of your increase to all persons with legitimate needs. When you give you are to give as if you were giving to Jesus himself. (Matt. 25:31-46.) This teaching is for everyone who comes into God's kingdom through salvation in Jesus. In obedience to His lordship, we are to use our unique abilities to gain by trading, to be faithful over what we gain and expect more, to recover any losses and then to give more and more. We are never to be without an abundance. This is what Jesus taught for everyone in His kingdom to *expect* and do.

All that call on the name of the Lord Jesus, asking Him to forgive them and to save them from the punishment of their sins, shall be saved (Acts 2:21; Rom. 10:13) and enter into His Plan of Flowing Wealth. If you do not have the assurance of salvation through Jesus Christ, ask Him to save you and be included in His plan to bless those who call upon the name of the Lord.

Heaven Responds to Faithfulness Over Material Wealth

Abraham was the *first* man since Adam's fall *who possessed* what God freely gave him and then faithfully ruled over the material possessions on behalf of the Lord. He was tenacious and determined not to lose what God had given him, but to *increase* it instead. He understood that God wanted him to be rich, and he wanted only God to have credit for making him rich. As heirs of Abraham, we must have this same attitude in order to have the benefits Abraham had.

Genesis 13:2 confirms that Abraham was already wealthy in livestock, silver and gold when the evil kings stole from him. He defeated them, not only recovering what he lost but much more. The king of Sodom made the offer to Abraham that he could keep the goods he had recovered while rescuing his nephew Lot, but Abraham replied, **I will not take from a thread even to a shoelachet, and that I will not take any thing that is thine, lest thou shouldest say, I have made Abram rich** (Gen. 14:23). He faithfully gave God the glory for his victory and wealth.

After Abraham maintained what God had given him and then worshipped Him by giving the tithe, a tenth of all he had gained in the war with the kings, God responded with His covenant blessings.

After these things the word of the Lord came unto Abram in a vision, saying, Fear not, Abram: I am thy shield, and thy exceeding great reward.
Genesis 15:1

Abraham fulfilled the spiritual law of *possessing* what was given to him. He consistently maintained what he was to rule over and did not make excuses for loss. He did not say, "God gave me great wealth but the evil kings stole it so now I have nothing." Instead he had faith in God and ruled over what was given to him by recovering what was taken.

Abraham was considered *righteous* in the eyes of God. He possessed the land God gave him and protected and guarded what was his. This is obedience to God's command to rule over material possessions, a command He gave Adam in the garden. God reveals this principle throughout His Word, and this is the spiritual principle that *Jesus taught* in Matthew 25:14-46.

Jesus taught that the master would bless those who had been faithful over what was given to them with even more. Jesus is the Lord of the kingdom Who will bless us with an increase for being faithful over the possessions He gives us

63

and for using the abilities we have to gain even more for His work. In this same way, Abraham was blessed with an increase when he was faithful over what was given to his family by recovering their great wealth stolen by the kings.

Abraham Received the Promise of Increase

When Abraham victoriously repossessed what was taken from him, the priest of the Most High God, Melchizedek, brought bread and wine to bless him. Abraham, who was faithful over God's material possessions in the earth, was personally blessed by the priest of the Most High of heaven. Melchizedek confirmed that it was God who had delivered Abraham's enemies into his hand, enabling him to recover what was stolen.

Satan is our enemy who comes to steal and destroy what God has given us, but Jesus is our Lord who will deliver our enemy into our hands so that our possessions from the Father can be recovered. Likewise, we need a *plan* of action like Abraham's.

In Matthew 25:14-30, Jesus illustrates how the lord of the kingdom personally blessed all those who were faithful over the master's wealth. Melchizedek personally appeared to bless Abraham for his faithfulness in the same way the lord of the kingdom blessed the faithful servants in chapter 25. What Jesus taught would happen to faithful stewards happened to Abraham.

We know Melchizedek was sent from heaven by the Most High God to personally bless Abraham with promises of much more to come. Melchizedek said to Abraham, **Blessed be Abram of the most high God, possessor of heaven and earth (Gen. 14:19).**

Can you understand what happened here? The priest of the Most High God came to personally bless faithful Abraham and said the *possessor of heaven and earth* had blessed him. This is the *first time* heaven had been able to say this since the fall of Adam.

God delegated the possession of the earth to man, who was to be under His control. God now must possess the earth *through man* or he does not possess the earth at all. Psalm 115:16 says the heavens are the Lord's, but the earth He has given to the children of men. As long as Adam was under God's control, he kept God's environment in the earth under control. When man controls the earth the way Jesus taught, then the earth is controlled for God's purposes.

God does not bless the unfaithful servant who will not increase or who allows God's blessings to be taken by the enemy. To decrease is to let Satan take away what rightfully is God's, just like he took it from Adam. To neither increase nor plan to gain is to let Satan keep what God wants you to legally gain by honest trade. We defeat Satan as we reclaim what is ours through the promises of God and as we worship God with the tithe (ten percent) of the increase.

If we refuse to rule over material wealth, we are allowing Satan to keep control of God's goods. If we refuse to gain by trading, we are turning our back on God's plan to possess the earth and provide for the needs of every man through His abundance. If we refuse to work with God in regaining and controlling the earth's wealth, we allow Satan to keep God's abundance from man just as he has tried to do since his first deception with Adam.

Abraham possessed the land through faith in God, the way God had told mankind to do it. This is why God sent the priest of heaven to bless Abraham and make him to be a ruler over much, promising his seed "the earth for their possession" (Rom. 4:13 AP).

As believers in Jesus Christ, we are heirs to God's covenant with Abraham. Galatians 3:26-29 teaches, *You are all the children of God though faith in Christ Jesus...if you belong to Christ, then you are Abraham's seed, and heirs according to the promise.* All who have faith in Jesus Christ are blessed along with Abraham.

Jesus Christ redeemed us from the curse of the law by being made a curse for us [on the cross of Calvary]. (Gal.3:13.) Because He redeemed us, the blessing given to Abraham can come to us through faith in Christ. We too can receive the promise of the Spirit of God. (Gal. 3:14.)

As we are faithful to *repossess* the promise of God through faith in Christ, God will repossess the earth through us as He did through Abraham's faith. The same promise to Abraham will be ours and God will be our shield and our exceeding great reward. (Gen. 15:1.)

Firstfruits From the Increase Glorify God

Abraham gave a tenth of all he had to Melchizedek, the priest of the Most High God. As we give from the firstfruits of our increase to the Lord, we worship God the way Abraham did. God has not asked us to worship with the firstfruits of the decrease. When God placed man over the earth, He commanded him to be fruitful, *multiply,* replenish and subdue the earth. Man was to *increase* all that was good in God's earth and he was to keep it for God, in the same way God would keep it.

When we *worship* with the firstfruits of the increase, Jesus, the Most High Priest of heaven, takes it, worships the Father with it and blesses us for being lords over it for Him. He says, "Well done, you good and faithful servant; you have been faithful over My earth. I will make you ruler over many things; enter into the joy of the Lord."

This promise is to all believers who are willing to possess and rule over the possessions God has given to them. The Lord expects us to benefit from His promises and wants us to take those promises into the marketplace of life, where we can trade with those promises for the needs of mankind and gain souls and riches for God's work to continue.

When you worship God with the first part of the increase (the tenth of all you have, like Abraham did), something very *special* happens. You become *partners* with God in *controlling* the wealth of the earth for His purposes. The Priest of heaven, Who is the Lord Jesus, receives it with joy. The Lord invites us to share His joy when we are faithful over the distribution of His wealth. He then gives His joy and blessings to us as we continue to increase and give to Him.

It pleases God when His servants in the earth are obedient to keep the wealth of the earth available for His purposes. Obedient servants accumulate wealth legally by trading and gaining and then through maintaining control over the increase with God's power and ability.

God *celebrates* when we are obedient to His command to be fruitful and multiply. He rejoices when we reclaim the wealth of the earth for His purposes. God has given His people "the power to get wealth, that He might establish his covenant which He swore to Abraham." (Deut. 8:18.) We draw on that power through faith in Christ and through the use of our abilities to gain by trading for profit with our goods and services.

The Greek word translated "ability" in Matthew 25:15 is *dunamis*, which is the power of the Holy Spirit. That means Jesus gives believers the power of the Holy Spirit, the same power that raised Jesus from the dead, to get wealth, to gain and to trade. Not only does He command us to take what He has given us and increase it, but He provides the supernatural power of His Spirit for us to do it!

5
Refusing Wealth Is Refusing God's Blessing

Jesus frequently taught about the appropriate use of money. Luke 19:1-10 records the story of how Zacchaeus was changed by an encounter with Jesus and became a person who used his wealth to provide for the poor. Zacchaeus was a wealthy man who was obviously disliked by the townspeople. He so desperately wanted to see who Jesus was that he ran ahead and climbed a tree to hear and see Him. Jesus walked to the tree, looked up and said to him, **Zacchaeus, make haste, and come down; for today I must abide at thy house** (Luke 19:5).

The rich man received Jesus with great joy, while many religious people criticized Jesus for giving such personal attention to a sinner. Zacchaeus said to Jesus, **Behold, Lord, the half of my goods I give to the poor; and if I have taken any thing from any man by false accusation, I restore to him fourfold** (v. 8). Jesus then said to him, **This day is salvation come to this house, forsomuch as he** [Zacchaeus] **also is a son of Abraham** (v. 9). Zacchaeus had gained and maintained and now, because he believed and received Jesus, he gave to the Lord like Abraham had.

While many stood listening to the conversation between Jesus and this wealthy man who had just promised to give to the poor and restore what he had gained unfairly, Jesus immediately began teaching the Principle of Gaining by Trading as a way of bringing the kingdom of God to earth by putting money to work for the master's use. This time we clearly see the parallel between the nobleman who travelled to a distant country to have himself appointed king and Jesus, who was preparing to leave earth for heaven and return later as our long-awaited King of kings.

Jesus illustrated how we are to use our money until He returns. Verse 11 tells that He is teaching this because many of His followers believed the kingdom of God was going to appear in the earth at once. Believers were thinking that God would immediately establish His kingdom as it is in heaven and rule over the earth with His justice (like He will at the end of time). But Jesus was teaching in this parable that *until* the end of time came, *God's way* of establishing His kingdom on earth is for every believer to use their abilities to *gain by trading* and then give to the needs of the people in His name.

Jesus was teaching us to put our *money to work* by using our abilities and business skills the way Abraham and Zacchaeus had. Zacchaeus knew how to *gain* but now, after receiving Jesus, he learned to *give.* The people to whom Jesus was telling the story seemed to understand how to give, but they were *not* applying the Principle of Gaining by Trading, because Jesus was emphasizing again that faithful servants are to *use* their money and gain with it.

Some people are still hoping that God will supernaturally take over the earth and put the wealth of sinners in their righteous control. (Prov. 13:22.) They serve God religiously but do not think they have to work and trade to get wealth. They think giving and following Jesus everywhere is the only part of God's Plan of Flowing Wealth.

Jesus told those who want to see the kingdom of God on earth to administrate His grace and power by distributing wealth to the poor. But in order to give wealth, we must first gain it. And we gain by trading what we have—our service skills, craft or product.

In Luke 19, Jesus retold the story (as in Matthew 25:14-30) of how the faithful servants traded with the money that their master had given them and were expected to gain an increase with what they were given.

Jesus was telling those who could understand His parable that until He returned as king, everyone who followed Him must actively *put their money to use* on His behalf and gain in order to give. Zacchaeus learned it wasn't scriptural to gain and not give, but we are also to learn that it isn't scriptural to give and not gain.

And as they heard these things, he added and spake a parable, because he was nigh to Jerusalem, and because they thought that the kingdom of God should immediately appear.

He said therefore, A certain nobleman went into a far country to receive for himself a kingdom, and to return.

And he called his ten servants, and delivered them ten pounds, and said unto them Occupy till I come.

But his citizens hated him, and sent a message after him, saying, We will not have this man to reign over us.

And it came to pass, that when he was returned, having received the kingdom, then he commanded these servants to be called unto him, to whom he had given the *money*, that he might know how much every man had gained by trading.

Then came the first, saying, Lord, thy pound hath *gained* ten pounds.

And he said unto him, Well, thou good servant: because thou hast been faithful in a very little, have thou authority over ten cities.

And the second came, saying, Lord, thy pound hath gained five pounds.

And he said likewise to him, Be thou also over five cities.

And another came, saying, Lord, behold, here is thy pound, which I have kept laid up in a napkin:

> For I feared thee, because thou art an austere man: thou takest up that thou layedst not down, and reapest that thou didst not sow.
>
> And he saith unto him, Out of thine own mouth will I judge thee, thou wicked servant. Thou knewest that I was an austere man, taking up that I laid not down, and reaping that I did not sow:
>
> Wherefore then gavest not thou my money into the bank, that at my coming I might have required mine own with usury?
>
> And he said unto them that stood by, Take from him the pound, and give it to him that hath ten pounds.
>
> (And they said unto him, Lord, he hath ten pounds.)
>
> For I say unto you, That unto *every one which hath shall be given*; and from him that hath not, even that he hath shall be taken away from him.
>
> But those mine enemies, which would not that I should reign over them, bring hither, and slay them before me.
>
> **Luke 19:11-27**

Immediately following the telling of this story, Jesus prepared for His triumphal entry into Jerusalem. He was preparing to go to heaven to have Himself appointed King, just as the nobleman in the parable went to a far country to become king. The parallel of the nobleman to Jesus is obvious. *We* believers are the servants in the story who are to "occupy" until He returns again. (v. 13.) *Strong's Exhaustive Concordance* defines *occupy* as "to busy oneself with trade," and *The New International Version* translates the verse, **Put this *money to work* until I come back.**

The emphasis of this story is that until Jesus Christ returns as King, we are to let Him be ruler over us by gaining and trading, then give to others. This will maintain the *balance* of God's Plan for Flowing Wealth and finance the ministry of Jesus throughout the earth.

Gain by Trading Until Jesus Comes

The kingdom Principle of Gaining by Trading in order to give is *expected* of all disciples. Zacchaeus illustrated the giving part of the principle, and Jesus reinforced the gaining part of God's Plan for Flowing Wealth.

Jesus also emphasized that those who will not obey by working and gaining are saying to Him, "We will not allow You to be our King and rule over us." (Luke 19:14 AP.) They are saying that they do not want to put their *money to work* on His behalf until He returns as King. In verse 27 Jesus reveals, "Those who refuse to allow Me to rule over them are enemies of the kingdom." By that, *they refuse to gain by trading*, to occupy until He returns.

Many believers have been ignorant of this Principle of Gaining by Trading, and some believers are in rebellion against God's plan to prosper His people in order to let His abundance flow for evangelism. We must *learn* to apply this teaching of Jesus, our Lord, so His kingdom is financially successful while we wait for His return as King.

To refuse to gain is to refuse to do things exactly Jesus' way. Refusing His way and His rule over us makes us His enemy and *hinders* the work of God. Let us rather advance His work in the earth by *obeying* whatever Jesus wants done.

> **And it came to pass, that when he was returned, having received the kingdom, then he commanded these servants to be called unto him, to whom he had given the money, that he might know *how much every man had gained by trading.*
> Luke 19:15**

Jesus is emphatically teaching that faithful servants gain by trading and bring the increase to Him.

6
Luke's Account of Gaining by Trading

Immediately following the conversion of Zacchaeus, Jesus taught the parable of gaining by trading (Luke 19:11). The people who were listening to the conversation Jesus was having with Zacchaeus thought that the kingdom of God would immediately appear. Jesus was illustrating that the kingdom would not appear the way they thought, but they could operate the principles of His kingdom by following the example of the faithful servants.

Jesus wants us to gain by trading until He comes again at the end of time. This is a vital and *expected* part of every Christian's life. The purpose of this teaching seems to clearly say, "*Every Christian* is expected to gain by trading until Jesus comes again."

The nobleman in verses 12 and 13 of Luke 19 did basically what the lord in Matthew 25:14-30 did. This time, however, Jesus tells of ten servants instead of three, and He said each of the servants was given the same amount of *money*. They was given one pound of money each, with the instructions, **Occupy till I come**, which means, "Stay in control of My possessions like I would until I return. Run My business exactly like I would until I get back."

His citizens hated the lord, saying, "We will not have this man [the lord] to rule over us." This means, we will not do things his way or according to his lordship. When he returned, he called *each* of his servants to whom he had given *money* and asked them how much they had *gained by trading*. Both times Jesus told this parable, *every man* was questioned. In each instance the master wanted to know what was *gained by trading*.

The first servant said, "Lord, your pound has gained ten pounds" or one thousand percent. The nobleman said, "Well done, you good servant: because you have been faithful in a very little [to gain by trading what I gave you], have authority over ten cities." Having authority over ten cities is a challenging amount of material wealth to be over. But Jesus spoke of huge amounts of material wealth in His examples of what He had in mind for those who followed Him. We are to gain by trading, and we are to faithfully keep and maintain what we gain for distribution in His kingdom work.

In verses 18 and 19, the second servant gained five pounds with the pound of money from the nobleman. This was a five hundred percent increase over what the lord had given him. His lord rewarded him by giving him five cities over which he was given authority to rule. The servant was to govern and rule over the cities to make them increase on behalf of the lord.

Be Master of Money for the Master

If money slips from you without a purposeful plan, for whatever good or bad reason, it is ruling you and you are not ruling it. Make up your mind that, in Jesus' name, you are the boss of the material wealth you have. It does not matter how small the amount is that you have now.

You are to govern the use of the money you have on behalf of the kingdom of God. The responsibility is on you to increase and maintain control of the increase. The increase can't leave your possession unless you let it. You are to be the boss over that money; you are to be in control. Money is ruling you if you let money go where it wants to.

Jesus teaches that as a servant of God you are to be in control of what He has given you. He has commanded you to increase and maintain for Him.

When your money says, "I want to get away from you in exchange for an eighty-cent piece of candy!" be the master over your money and say, "No!" Then find a way to have the candy and keep the money by taking that eighty cents past the corner store, which charges high prices for the convenience of sweets, to a wholesale or to a discount store, where you can buy many more sweets for half the price.

You can increase your eighty cents for the Lord of the kingdom by using it to make more money and still enjoy what is pleasing and good for food. Eat sweets from the profit of selling half of the candy that you buy at wholesale prices to people who are willing to pay more for convenience.

Don't work for money, make it work for you. Don't be bribed by convenience. You can make money reproduce itself by *planning* for an increase. You can eat sweets free of charge by smart buying and selling, which makes it possible for you to maintain the eighty cents, eat candy and have more money than you started with to give to the Lord of the kingdom. Be obedient to use your money *wisely.* It may take more planning to buy at the wholesale store, but you will be rewarded by having the candy and increasing your investment at the same time.

Who is the boss of your money? Be the ruler over your money for Jesus. Use what money you have to increase for God in obedience to the teachings of Jesus. Tell your money, "I work for Jesus, you work for me and we will increase for Him."

This is how the principle of gaining by trading works in order to release God's Plan of Flowing Wealth into His kingdom. This is how the kingdom of God should operate in the earth until Jesus returns. We are to serve God by making money work and increasing it for meeting the needs of others.

Be the master of money for the Master! Don't let your money leave because it wants its freedom in exchange for the bribe of convenience. Be the ruler over your money and increase your wealth through wise spending, trading, gaining, maintaining and giving on behalf of the Lord.

In verses 20 through 23, the servant who did not increase had various reasons why he did not gain. The lord was displeased and called him "wicked" for not increasing. Again, we see Jesus teaching, "You should have at least put the money in the bank so it would have increased with the interest." (AP.)

Then the lord said to those who stood nearby, "Take away what the wicked servant has and give it to the one who has increased the most." The other servants seem to argue with the lord, "But, he has ten pounds." Then in verse 26 the lord explains the principle of increase and decrease, which is so important for every follower of Jesus to understand: **Unto** *every one which hath shall be given;* **and from him that hath not, even that he hath shall be taken away from him.**

Jesus made it very plain that the servants who refused to allow the lord to rule over them and were not obedient to gain and maintain the way the lord of the kingdom had told them were enemies. The lord said, "But those mine enemies, which would not that I should reign over them, bring here and slay before me."

According to the teaching of Jesus, this is what awaits the servants of the kingdom who *refuse* to gain by trading and *maintain* control over what they have gained for the lord of the kingdom.

The emphasis in verse 27 is that those who refuse to let the Lord reign over them will be punished. Those who refuse to do what the Lord says to do become enemies of the Lord. Being slain before the Lord for not gaining, maintaining, and giving seems very drastic to me. But gaining and ruling over material possessions has traditionally been *minimized,* neglected and even taught against by the church. Perhaps drastic measures are required to implement this important teaching of Jesus to gain by trading and give to His work until He comes again.

To gain is to let Jesus reign, and to gain places you in a position to receive His favorable response of, "Well done, good and faithful servant. You have been faithful over little; I will make you ruler over many things." (Luke 19:27; Matt. 25:21,23 AP.)

The Wealth Transfer Plan

A good man leaveth an inheritance to his children's children: and the wealth of the sinner is laid up for the just.

Proverbs 13:22

God's plan is for the wealth of the wicked to be put into the hands of the just. The supernatural transfer of the earth's riches into the hands of the righteous will not come until Jesus returns as King. *Yet, legal transfers of wealth into the hands of believers should be occurring all the time in their business dealings.* As you *market* your goods and services for an increase, you should expect successful gain, because you are in obedience to Jesus' Plan for Flowing Wealth to come into His control through *your obedience* to Him.

Your obedience to His teaching of gaining by trading will put the wealth into your hands. This removes the *mystery* of how we will have the money to give to the needs of others. Jesus explained how we can bring finances into the kingdom right after Zacchaeus promised to give from the wealth he had already gained.

Continual gaining and giving, giving and gaining is the key to God's Plan of Flowing Wealth to finance the ministry of the kingdom. To be slack in either giving or gaining cripples the work of the kingdom. Be obedient to do precisely what Jesus taught concerning both.

2000 Years of Poverty Was Not God's Plan

If the people who were expecting the kingdom of heaven to immediately appear and the wealth of the wicked to be supernaturally transferred to the hands of the just were still alive today, they would be empty-handed and waiting, for the time of transfer has still not come.

Two thousand years of poverty is not God's way for His servants. He wants the kingdom of heaven to come to earth by allowing Jesus to work through us, directing us in how to gain by trading and give to His kingdom work. This is God's Plan of Flowing Wealth now and has been His plan of transfer since the foundation of the earth.

7

The Widow Gained by Trading

An associate pastor died, leaving his wife and family in serious debt. This is not an uncommon situation, but this story demonstrates God's Plan for Flowing Wealth for widows and orphans. This bereaved wife and mother called the senior pastor and informed him of the seriousness of the financial crisis. She told him that it was so serious, her children were about to be taken away until her debt was satisfied.

The senior pastor seemed somewhat insensitive to helping the widow pay the debt, which was incurred by his very faithful assistant minister who had died. He asked the destitute mother what she had in her house that could go toward paying off the debt. All she had was a small jar of oil.

Now you would think the senior minister would immediately supply finances from the church "emergency or benevolence fund" until he could receive an offering from the church members for the destitute mother and children. After all, her faithful husband had been a minister of their church. You would think the deacons and congregation, who were so faithfully cared for by the assistant minister and his wife, would now be summoned to minister to her needs. But this seemingly insensitive senior minister does not offer to even have the members of the church bring a covered-dish meal. By the way he is botching up this job of caring for his deceased assistant's wife and kids, he appears to know nothing of the compassionate ways of God.

He gives no personal assistance to help her in her bereaved dilemma. All he offers is what seems to be uncompassionate, unrelated advice to the present crisis. The first statement he makes is, "What do you have in the house to satisfy this debt which is so great that your creditors have a legal right to take your kids?" She tells him of the single jar of oil. The next even less encouraging instruction from the senior minister is, "Send your children to borrow as many empty containers as they can find. When they return, shut your door and poor oil into all the containers and set them to one side."

Now this faithful assistant minister's wife could have said, "I told you I only have a small amount of oil! With what will I fill the other containers? I must have more information about what you plan to do after we have borrowed these containers." She could have said, "I don't believe in borrowing. The Scripture says: 'Owe no man anything but to love him.' So I don't believe in borrowing. And besides, I think you are callous in not helping us in our hour of great need." She could have said, "I don't believe in a cluttered house, especially at this time of great grief. I don't want empty containers all over my living room." She could have said, "This is no way to treat the children, since they have just lost their daddy. I don't want my children to look like they are begging."

She could have taken offense by what the senior minister had asked her to do. She could have been discouraged that he seemed so unwilling to relieve her very real pain and was compounding an already desperate situation. She had called the senior minister for answers, and he was only giving limited instructions, which seemed to add responsibilities without relieving the pressure of her need for help.

This lady had good reason to be upset by the unorthodox manner in which her terrible crisis was being handled in such an uncharitable way. Charity and compassion had been a way of life for her and her husband when they worked together in the ministry, and now it seems she is not receiving either from the senior minister. But she demonstrates faith, as though she understands there may be another solution to her dilemma besides total dependence on a charitable contribution from the church.

Refusing to be upset, she dutifully sends her children to borrow the many containers. Soon the vessels will clutter her normally well-kept house, in which she has often ministered to the needs of others. After her children return with borrowed containers, she obediently begins to fill them from her small jar.

It is challenging to start pouring the small amount of oil into a larger container, but her obedience is greatly rewarded. She observes the miracle of supply as her small jar of oil continues to fill all the containers her children had borrowed. She refused the many good reasons to be offended and obeyed what the senior pastor told her to do, even though he did not offer to do the work for her. As the widow obeyed the instructions of this man of God, every borrowed vessel was filled to overflowing.

When she finished filling all the containers, and when her house had vessels full of oil everywhere, she went to the senior minister for further instructions about her serious indebtedness. He gave only brief instructions and offered no further assistance in the added work he told her to do. He said, "Go sell the oil, and pay the debt, and you and your children live on what is left of the *money you make* selling the oil."

Still she is patient and does what he says, showing the graciousness of her charitable life. Up to now, much work has been done by her and her children, with no relief or promise of relief from the preacher or anyone. I admire the way this faithful minister's wife handled what seemed to be such unfair treatment from her pastor in a time of bereavement and desperate indebtedness. He seemed indifferent to the needs of this faithful, unselfish servant of God. His apathy would be more expected toward the needs of transient strangers, but this woman was a dedicated member of his pastoral team.

He was brief and without detailed explanation. He didn't volunteer to personally help her in any way: *EXCEPT, he gives her God's Plan for Flowing Wealth to finance her continued ministry, which Jesus taught in Matthew 25:14-30 and Luke 19:11-27.*

That's right! This minister, who seemed not to care, gives this lady in need of charity *the part* of the Plan for Flowing Wealth she and her minister husband had not yet used. They had practiced only the giving part of the plan and now they were in desperate lack, even though they were devoutly dedicated and in a prominent national ministry. They were associate ministers to the greatest man of faith and power in the history of ministry. This great senior minister had appeared to be insensitive, *but* he had given the widow the key to God's provision for financial success. This key is for *all* in the kingdom of God who will apply the *full formula* of both gaining and giving in balance.

This great man of God who advised the widow was Elisha. The story is found in 2 Kings 4:1-7. Elisha cared enough to teach this faithful minister's widow the principle of *balancing* her giving with gaining. He helped her learn to depend on God and to trade with whatever she had been given in order to gain the financial abundance she so desperately needed to continue her ministry as a mother and servant to the needs of others. Because she unselfishly served the church and was dedicated to her family, she was deserving of the blessing. But she had to put her faith into action in order to see God's abundant provision for her needs.

Elisha gave the widow the Principle of Gaining by Trading that God wants each of His dedicated children to apply in their ministry. We are to look to God's abundant supply when we see the charitable needs of others. We can meet those needs in His name, to His glory, if we will look for His provision. He has given each of us something with which we can trade and gain a financial increase. God will abundantly bless us when we obediently respond to *all* His instructions. (John 15:10-17.)

When the widow said, "The vessels are full," Elisha told her to *balance* abundant giving with gaining by trade. He told her to sell the oil, pay the debt, and live on the rest. This principle is exactly what Jesus taught later. Gaining by trade is half of the kingdom Principles of Gaining and Giving, and examples of this principle are found throughout the Word of God. Giving to the needs of others is the second part of the formula. The widow knew about giving, because her husband was a servant to Elisha. We know the servant was dedicated, giving his life to the work of the ministry, but obviously the widow and her husband did not foresee the need to plan for receiving.

Commitment to only the giving half of the formula for financial success will cause you to fail financially. You must be dedicated to consistent, abundant gaining and to consistent, abundant giving out of the firstfruits of your increase! Negligence in application of either principle of gaining or giving will put you out of balance in what Jesus taught as the formula for financing the successful ministry of the kingdom.

The Responsibility to Gain Enough

Consider the great responsibility Elisha put on the bereaved minister's wife by telling her to gain enough from the sales of her oil to pay all of her debts with enough to live on the rest. He does not tell her to sell enough to pay her debts. He sets a much higher goal for which she is held responsible. Elisha laid a responsibility on her to sell her oil for enough to live on after paying all her debts.

The aim of God's plan for abundant life through His divine principles is not for you to just get out of debt. God wants you to apply the Principle of Gaining by Trading so that you are out of debt and abundantly living on the rest! To gain by trading is exactly what God told Elisha to tell the faithful widow to do.

"Trust God for the increase, sell for more than it cost you, pay your debts and live on the rest and continue to be in a position that you can minister to the needs of others instead of begging bread yourself," is the moral of the story in 2 Kings 4:1-7. The profits for selling the oil were more than enough to just get the widow out of debt. She was no longer dependent on someone to provide for her. God provided for her so that she could fulfill her responsibilities as a mother and servant to the work of God.

Notice, instruction from God's prophet with God's plan for the lady is, "Sell for high profit." This story corresponds with Jesus' teaching about the lord of the kingdom who was pleased with the servants who had made great profit by selling. Big profit, honestly made by creative marketing and planning, is emphasized both in the story of the widow and the parables of Matthew 25 and Luke 19.

Oil was a common product, so to be obedient to the instruction of selling for high profit, the widow had to be creative and prayerful on how and where to market. Perhaps her creative marketing was to offer free delivery, direct to the customer's door, in order to make her product more appealing to her buyers. We do know she had been given the responsibility from God to make the most of her product by applying the kingdom Principle of Gaining by Trading. God blessed the widow for her faith, obedience and trust in the Word of God given to her through the prophet, Elisha.

Trade Secrets, Miracles and Borrowing

God taught *trade secrets* to this dedicated lady of ministry. She was told by Elisha, "When you come to your house with all the borrowed vessels, shut the door upon you and your sons and pour the oil into all the vessels" (2 Kings 4:4 AP). He was telling the widow and her sons to *privately* prepare their product for market. Keep your trade secret. Do not let the world know how little you gave for what you are about to sell for full market value. They will not give you the price you deserve, the true market value, if they know how little you gave for it. It's not the world's business to know how little you paid for your product.

God makes financial blessings possible for you when you trust Him to get you out of debt. He wants to teach you how to have abundant life. Never lie about your product, but be strong and *keep* your trade secrets just as God taught this lady. Gaining by trading is for *all* people of the kingdom. To make the big profits, in obedience to kingdom teaching, trade secrets are not only important, they are imperative!

Some believers feel it is wrong to *borrow,* but if this lady had not believed in borrowing, her miracle of supernatural debt-elimination would not have taken place. If she had not believed in *miracles,* she would not have been out of debt, either. It took faith to collect the jars and begin to pour the oil. If she had only believed in giving and not in *selling,* her miracle of supernatural debt-elimination would not have taken place. Borrowing, the miraculous provision of a product, and selling to the market were all necessary to bring her out of this home-wrecking, debt crisis. Unbelief in any of the three steps of wise marketing principles would have kept her a pauper and her sons in slavery for the rest of their days.

The instructions were to borrow all the vessels possible. Most likely, this lady was not accustomed to the business practices of borrowing, keeping trade secrets, and selling for high profit. But she cleared her debt by trading for gain with a common product which many others were selling in her area.

Borrowing was the first step this lady was asked to take. She obeyed the divine instruction on how to get out of her financial crisis and into God's abundance. God supplied the marketable product that she needed, but the extent of her miracle depended on her capacity to borrow. When the last of the many borrowed vessels was filled, her supernatural supply of a marketable product stopped. She was instructed in verse 3 to go borrow all the vessels she could, and not just a few. When the last borrowed vessel was filled, the oil stopped flowing. The oil did not stop before the last borrowed vessel was used, but when the extent of her borrowing was reached the provision stopped.

The Bible does not teach against borrowing. Jesus said, **Give to him that asketh thee, and from him that would borrow of thee turn not thou away** (Matt. 5:42). The ideal is to reach the place where you are "the head and not the tail." By obeying God, you can be blessed in all you put your hands to. The ideal is to reach the place in financial gain where you lend unto many and not borrow.

> **The Lord shall open unto thee his good treasure, the heaven to give the rain unto thy land in his season, and to bless all the work of thine hand: and thou shalt lend unto many nations, and thou shalt not borrow.**
>
> **And the Lord shall make thee the head, and not the tail; and thou shalt be above only, and thou shalt not be beneath; if that thou hearken unto the commandments of the Lord thy God, which I command thee this day, to observe and to do them:**

> **And thou shalt not go aside from any of the words**
> **which I command thee this day, to the right hand, or to**
> **the left, to go after other gods to serve them.**
> **Deuteronomy 28:12-14**

If God was against borrowing, He would not bring you to the place of lending unto many. He wants you to apply the financial Principle of Gaining by Trading (by selling your goods and services) so you will not need to borrow. He wants you to be so blessed by gaining and giving that you can lend unto many and not have to borrow from anyone. He wants to be your source of supply.

As you gain abundantly by trading, apply the *proper borrowing principle* that Elisha taught the bankrupt widow. She did not borrow for pleasure, living expenses, or to pay off some of her past-due bills. She did not borrow to upgrade her lifestyle to a more pleasurable position. Her sole purpose in borrowing was to put her product for sale on the market at a large profit. What she borrowed made it possible to have a product to sell for profit. She did not live off of or pay bills with what she borrowed. She produced and sold a product with what was borrowed. Her instructions were to sell the product, pay her debt and live on the rest. (2 Kings 4:1-7.)

I believe the instructions given to this destitute woman are some divine principles of borrowing:

• Limit borrowing only for the business purpose of putting your product or service in the marketplace.

• Sell the product for a great profit.

• Pay your debts from the increase you gain.

• Live off of a percentage of the profit.

• Do not live off the percentage of what is borrowed.

The widow whose husband served Elisha should have known of God's Word concerning borrowing. The instructions to Israel in Deuteronomy had been in writing since the days of Moses, and being a woman of ministry, she knew the Word of God. But the specifics of the proper motive for borrowing were not known to her until divine revelation came through Elisha. This divine revelation is written in the Bible to us now. We can see by Deuteronomy 28:12 that the ideal is to reach the place of lending instead of borrowing. By the instructions of 2 Kings 4:3, we can see that we can borrow enough to put our profit-making product on the market until we accomplish the ideal of lending to many and never borrowing.

Borrowing should only be a temporary necessity. With consistent gaining by trading and by ruling over the increase, we will reach a place of blessing where we will be the one to give to others. This is the plan of God concerning His people.

As you apply the biblical Principle of Gaining by Trading, you will get out of your financial disaster. Remember, we know the widow was already a giver because she and her husband were servants to the prophet. But she needed to know how to gain in order to have a *balanced* understanding of God's Plan for Flowing Wealth. More than likely, you have been taught to give but have not been shown God's plan for you to also gain. Thank God He has now revealed both the gaining and giving parts of His plan. You can't be stopped from winning as you diligently apply what God's Word teaches about the *balance* of gaining and giving.

All Christians should be using the divine principles taught to this distraught mother, those which Jesus later taught for all of His faithful followers. Be faithful to gain with the little you have, and apply the divine principle of ruling over the increase for God, and you too will see the miracle of abundance pouring into your life!

8
Joseph the Faithful Servant

Joseph was the first of Abraham's descendants who faithfully followed the same Principles of Gaining and Giving that had brought success to his legendary great-grandfather. He was the eleventh son of Jacob and Abraham's first great-grandson to prosper to the magnitude that Abraham had prospered. Joseph's success came because he diligently listened to the voice and Word of God. Joseph, like Abraham, *expected* God to prosper him in everything he obediently put his hand to.

To fully appreciate Joseph's story, I encourage you to read chapters 37 through 50 in the book of Genesis. In Genesis 17 you will read of God's promise to be Abraham's God and the God of his descendants and to make him and his heirs exceedingly fruitful. In return, Abraham and his heirs were to obey the covenant. In Genesis 22:17, God told Abraham that, because of his obedience, his descendents would take possession of the cities of their enemies and all nations would be blessed through his offspring.

As believers, we are heirs of God's promises to Abraham through our faith in Jesus Christ. God's covenant to make Abraham's descendants fruitful and heirs of His promises is for *all* who obey His commands. Galations 3:29 NIV teaches, **If you belong to Christ, then you are Abraham's seed, and heirs according to the promise.** This means we are the children of Abraham with a right to the exact blessings that God promised to Abraham's descendants.

All believers receive this covenant promise, but the principles which make it work must be applied. We do not receive the benefits just because we are heirs to Abraham. We must *believe* in the promises of God and *be obedient* to His commands. The covenant promises only worked for Abraham when he demonstrated faith and obeyed the voice and Word of God. His confidence in God caused him to expect success in whatever God instructed him to do. As heirs to the promises, we must show belief in the same way Abraham did.

But without faith it is impossible to please him; for he that cometh to God must believe that he is, and that he is a rewarder of them that diligently seek him.
Hebrews 11:6

Joseph Prospers in All He Does

The Lord was with Joseph and he had great spiritual communion with the Lord because he consistently obeyed the voice and the Word of God as Abraham had. His ten older brothers had the same opportunity and right to the covenant, but unlike Joseph, they were not faithul to seek God's plan to secure these promises.

The Lord proclaimed through Moses, in Deuteronomy 28:1-14, all the blessings that would come upon those who hearkened diligently unto the *voice* of the Lord and who faithfully obeyed all His commands.

The Lord will grant you abundant prosperity — in the fruit of your womb, the young of your livestock and the crops of your ground — in the land he swore to your forefathers to give you.

The Lord will open the heavens, the storehouse of his bounty, to send rain on your land in season and to bless all the work of your hands. You will lend to many nations but will borrow from none. The Lord will make you the head, not the tail. If you pay attention to the commands of the Lord your God that I give you this day

and carefully follow them, you will always be at the top, never at the bottom. Do not turn aside from any of the commands I give you today, to the right or to the left, following other gods and serving them.
Deuteronomy 28:11-14 NIV

These scriptures give both the conditions for being blessed and the promises of prosperity that become yours when you obey God's commands. This same covenant which God made with Abraham was revealed and recorded by Moses five hundred years after Abraham lived. These conditions and promises were evident in the life of Abraham and in his descendants even before Moses wrote them down in Deuteronomy 28:1-14.

We can clearly see the application of these principles in the life of Joseph and the absence of them in the lives of his ten older brothers. Joseph experienced the spiritual and the natural blessings of God when his brothers did not, because he consistently sought God just as his great-grandfather, Abraham, had done.

Joseph prospered more than his brothers because he was meeting the conditions explained in Deuteronomy 28. God prospered Joseph, blessed his work, and made him the head and not the tail, above only and not beneath. Even when Joseph was young, he prospered more than his brothers and had experiences with God that his brothers did not have. Because of his dedicated lifestyle to do things God's way, Joseph prospered spiritually, physically and materially even when his brothers did not.

Joseph Prospers With a Better Job and Royal Clothes

Joseph was given distinction and a royal coat of honor by his father, Jacob, and his brothers were not. You may think that Jacob favored his youngest son because Joseph was the child of his old age (Gen. 37:3), but his younger brother, Benjamin, was not given a royal coat of distinction. The favor Joseph had must have been more than just being born late in his father's life.

God brought blessings and favor on Joseph in order to later bless the heirs of His inheritance. God blessed Joseph because he faithfully obeyed every task he was given to do. Joseph knew how to obediently trust God's ways and to give the glory back to Him for the provision.

For example, when later tempted to sin with Potiphar's wife, Joseph chose to obey God. (Gen. 39:9.) When tempted to take credit for the ability to interpret dreams, Joseph gave honor to God. (Gen. 41:16.) He diligently hearkened to God and expected God to make a way of provision for him. As a result, God commanded blessings and honor on him, as Deuteronomy 28:1-14 promises.

Joseph's father gave him a supervisory job over his older brothers, which was a better job than his brothers were given. In obedience to his father, wearing his coat of royal splendor and authority, he went to check on the activities of his older brothers. They had many reasons to envy Joseph. He was younger than all of them, yet was more royally dressed and was given the nonsweat job of keeping tabs on how well they were carrying out their father's orders. He was prospering above them. He had earned the right, not with their father, but with God.

Joseph Prospers in the Pit

Even when his brothers lowered him into the pit while they debated his fate, he prospered. There, he was in a cooler, more bickering-free place than the hot desert sand where his brothers were arguing! This was his pit stop, like that of a race car driver, while the pit crew (his brothers) sweated to get him on his way to win the race. (Gen. 37:23,24.)

His brothers could not harm him or destroy him. God prospered him in all he did. Even before they were through eating, rich merchants with a caravan of costly merchandise, aromatic perfumes and spices bought Joseph and took him to Egypt. His brothers thought they had put him in slavery, but *they had actually advanced his prosperity* by sending him to Egypt. He prospered in all his ways, no matter who was against him.

Joseph Prospers Over the Richest House in Egypt

Once Joseph was in Egypt, he was immediately purchased by Potiphar, the richest, most powerful man in the land and the captain of Pharaoh's elite, personal security force. **And the Lord was with Joseph and he was a prosperous man...And his master saw that the Lord was with him, and that the Lord made all that he did to prosper in his hand** (Gen. 39:2,3).

Again we see the promise of Deuteronomy 28:1-14 at work in Joseph's life. The promise is: The Lord will make it to prosper. He will command it to prosper, even in what appears to be disadvantaged situations.

Joseph served Potiphar, who put him in full charge of all his business. Potiphar's wife repeatedly tried to seduce Joseph, but he would not dishonor his master nor sin against God. (Gen. 39:9.) When Mrs. Potiphar could not successfully cause Joseph to compromise his diligence to God, she accused him of seducing her. Potiphar believed her and appeared to give Joseph a demotion by sending him to prison.

But you cannot demote a person who faithfully hearkens to the voice and Word of God. You cannot demote the person who has *expectant faith* in God's provision. The power to demote or prosper is not in man's hands. Through obedient faith, Joseph had earned the right to prosper in all he set his hands to; therefore, regardless of how bad things looked at the time for Joseph, God continued to prosper him. He didn't even defend himself against the accusations of Mrs. Potiphar. He just kept on serving God and was immediately "promoted."

Joseph Is Promoted to Prison

You may ask, "How could prison be a promotion?" God promises to prosper those who faithfully obey His commands, those who are expectant of His blessings and who trust Him without murmuring and complaining. Joseph was fully faithful, so prison became a promotion to greater prosperity than what Joseph had before. God honors His Word and prospers those who obey His commands.

Joseph's master, Potiphar, put him in the king's prison, where the king put his own servants when they offended him. It was not a place where hard criminals were kept. (Gen. 39:20.) The king's chief butler and chief baker were sent there, where Joseph was in charge. (Gen. 40:2.)

The Lord was with Joseph and the prison warden put Joseph in charge of all those held in the prison. Even in prison, Joseph faithfully tended the job he had been given. Again, he prospered more than all the others. The prison was a promotion in God's plan to prosper him.

Joseph diligently obeyed God with expectant faithfulness. The reward for faithfulness and obedience is prosperity in all you put your hands to. Joseph could not be demoted! He was faithful and diligent to rule over whatever situation was dealt to him.

The keeper of the prison trusted Joseph so much that he didn't even check on anyone who had been put under Joseph's care. Joseph had freedom even in prison, because the Lord was with him and made him prosper. (Gen. 39:22,23.)

Joseph was faithful to God and God was faithful to make a way for Joseph! The promise is, **The Lord shall** command the blessing upon thee in thy storehouses, and in all that thou settest thine hand unto; and he shall bless thee in the land which the Lord thy God giveth thee (Deut. 28:8). Even when it first appeared that God was failing to honor His Word to faithful Joseph, He was working to prosper him. God is always faithful, and He prospered Joseph regardless of where he was.

Two More Years of Prison Prosperity

After Joseph gave the meaning of their dreams to the chief butler and the chief baker, he continued to rule over the concerns of the prison. He remained in full control over his own freedom for two more years within the prison. Joseph's success increased with each step in his life. In each apparent demotion, he ended up more prosperous and with more responsibility than his previous assignment.

The butler had promised to tell Pharaoh about Joseph in exchange for Joseph's favor to interpret the chief butler's dream. Yet for two more years the butler did not remember Joseph to Pharaoh, until Pharaoh had two very serious dreams which no one could interpret.

At this time, the chief butler told Pharaoh of Joseph and his unique ability to interpret difficult, supernatural dreams. Immediately Pharaoh sent for Joseph. Joseph hastily shaved and changed his clothes. (In the royal fashion Joseph was accustomed to, he properly prepared himself in expensive raiment to be presented before Pharaoh.)

Pharaoh asked Joseph if he could interpret his dreams. Joseph answered, **It is not in me: God shall give Pharaoh an answer of peace** (Gen. 41:16). Joseph gave full credit to God and had full confidence that God would then give the interpretation. In faith, Joseph stated that God would interpret the dreams right then. Joseph enjoyed the type of relationship with God that people who are consistently diligent and hearken to the voice and the Word of God can expect. He had confidence that God would provide the answer in this time of need.

You can enjoy the same relationship that Joseph had with God by diligently seeking the voice of God and by obeying whatever He tells you to do. Begin early in the day by prayer and communion with Him. Then you will be aware of Him all through the day with the same intimacy and confidence that Joseph experienced.

Pharaoh told Joseph the dreams, and immediately Joseph interpreted them. He told Pharaoh that there would be seven years of great plenty on the earth followed by seven years of great lack caused by a terrible worldwide famine. The famine would be one of the worst ever known to man. It would devour all that was stored during the seven years of plenty. It would be a very grievous, world-shattering situation. Joseph made it plain that God was revealing to Pharaoh what was about to happen, so that Pharaoh could act in time to make provision for the people. (Gen. 41:25-32.)

Prospering Even in Great Famine Is Scriptural

Scripture reveals that you can prosper in a time of famine when you obey God and trust His Word. Joseph knew that prospering in a worldwide famine was God's will. Joseph knew his great-granddaddy Abraham and granddad Isaac had prospered in famine, because they hearkened to the voice and the *Word* of God. Knowing God wants to prosper His people in everything was part of Joseph's heritage from the Abrahamic covenant God had made with his forefathers.

With this godly belief in prosperity, Joseph was able to paint a picture of hope and provision to Pharaoh about the coming famine. Joseph revealed God's plan to save goods during the time of plenty in order to have supplies during the time of lack.

I am sure that the doomsday preachers of that time would have said, "This famine is from God. It is sent to straighten out the evil, pagan world of Pharaoh, so there is nothing you can do but to prepare for the suffering that must accompany this great drought. 'Prospering in everything you do,' may be found in the Word, but it doesn't mean prosperity in this famine, about which God has forewarned us. Remember, God said it would affect the whole world. Prepare to suffer, because this is 'The Big, Bad One' to straighten everyone out."

Well, Joseph wasn't a doom and gloom preacher. He was a Good News Preacher! He had heard from the Word of God and he knew through the historic reality of faith demonstrated by his forefathers that, regardless of famine, those who believe God's Word will receive the blessings that He promises. Those who have confidence in God will receive exactly what He promises to give.

Joseph believed that God forewarned them of the coming famine so they could prepare to live and not die during the impending crisis. Anyone who chose to believe God's Word had time to participate in His plan of salvation. We will look more fully at Joseph's storehouse plan of plenty for the coming famine in chapter 9.

Ruler Over Unlimited Plenty

The parables of the good stewards in Matthew 25 and Luke 19 reveal that faithfulness even over little assignments gives you mastery over much. God rewards those who apply this divine principle. Joseph had been faithful over every job he had been given to do, from truthfully reporting to his father the affairs of his older brothers to always telling others all God showed him. Joseph applied the principle of being a faithful servant everywhere he went, from Potiphar's house to the king's executive prison. Joseph was faithful to excel in whatever responsibilty was given to him, so increased responsibility was given to him.

Everywhere the Lord led him, Joseph was faithful over people, finances and responsibilities. Even in what appeared to be demotions, he remained faithful to oversee the tasks before him. Joseph never lost, and no one ever lost with Joseph. To turn things over to Joseph was to guarantee gain and success. This was established fact.

You will see in the next chapter how unlimited rulership over all Egypt was finally placed in Joseph's hands. When you are faithful to the voice and Word of God, God will make you the head and not the tail. (Deut. 28:13.)

The Head and Not the Tail by Divine Decree

God commanded a position of authority and blessing for Joseph everywhere he went because he was faithful to rule over all situations as he knew the Lord wanted them handled. He had overseen everything in God's name and for God. Pharaoh had never heard of this Hebrew slave before the day he searched for an interpretation of his dream, and after only moments in his presence, he put Joseph over all of Egypt. Pharaoh did this without the plan even being proven. As far as Pharaoh knew, Joseph could have been the greatest con artist in the history of the world.

Joseph's interpretation called for seven years of plenty before seven years of lack. It would take fourteen years to test this interpretation, and it is not a natural occurrence for a king to put a prisoner in charge of his entire economy! God had commanded that Joseph be established by His divine decree, which could not be altered by man. With or without a king, God honored His Word and made Joseph the head and not the tail in a totally pagan empire, because he was faithful over everything that God had put in his charge.

> And Pharaoh said unto his servants, Can we find such a one as this is, a man in whom the spirit of God is?

> And Pharaoh said unto Joseph, Forasmuch as God hath shewed thee all this, there is none so discreet and wise as thou art:

> Thou shalt be over my house, and according unto thy word shall all my people be ruled: only in the throne will I be greater than thou.

> And Pharaoh said unto Joseph, See, I have set thee over all the land of Egypt.

> And Pharaoh took off his ring from his hand, and put it upon Joseph's hand, and arrayed him in vestures of fine linen, and put a gold chain about his neck;

> And he made him to ride in the second chariot which he had; and they cried before him, Bow the knee: and he made him ruler over all the land of Egypt.

> And Pharaoh said unto Joseph, I am Pharaoh, and without thee shall no man lift up his hand or foot in all the land of Egypt.

> Genesis 41:38-44

Executive Benefits Accompany God's Plan of Prosperity

Not only was Joseph made Chief Executive Officer over the affairs of Egypt, but he immediately received top executive benefits. Joseph simply presented God's plan of plenty to Pharaoh, and *before the plan was even put on paper*, he was put in charge of the entire kingdom. Joseph had simply applied the same success principles of gaining an increase over what he had been given that he had previously applied in smaller situations.

Joseph boldly spoke the Word which God had given to him for Pharaoh. Now his obedience gained him the second most luxurious "limousine" in the nation, Pharaoh's personal Imperial Ring, an exquisite royal wardrobe and a gold chain which was placed around his neck by Pharaoh himself. Joseph also received the authority and resources of a pagan king who supported him in fulfilling the plan God had given him. (Gen. 41:42.)

As descendants of Abraham, we have received the same rights to success as Joseph received. With the plan of plenty that Jesus teaches, we can expect success when we are obedient to God's plan. Joseph didn't seek prosperity and success, but success followed him whenever he obeyed God. As he succeeded in all that God called him to do, he was also prosperous.

When God gives you His divine plan, He also gives you the authority and resources to back the plan. As you obey God's Plan of Flowing Wealth through gaining by trading and giving, you can expect the backing you need to carry out the plan and immediate benefits for your obedience. The increase happens after you are faithful to rule over smaller matters. God will give you more fruitful responsibilities when your efforts bear fruit in the smaller matters first.

Joseph had proven his faithfulness by the time he was thirty years old. (Gen. 41:46.) Let's review some of the principles that caused him to gain and succeed in all he put his hand to, including why Pharaoh put him in charge of Egypt.

• He was faithful over whatever assignment he was given and worked as unto the Lord, regardless of whether it was a task from his father, Potiphar, the prison warden or the Pharaoh.

• Joseph never lost, and no one ever lost with Joseph.

• He gave God the glory for the abilities God had given him.

- Joseph believed God's Word and followed His instructions exactly as he was told.

- He told others of God's plan and thereby spoke the Word of God into their lives so that it could be heeded.

Divine Plans Are Released Through Speaking God's Word

If Joseph had not told Pharaoh of God's plan, Pharaoh would not have known how to use his authority to prevent the impending disaster. Joseph boldly proclaimed God's plan. Pharaoh was so pleased with the Word of God spoken through Joseph, that he gave Joseph a royal wedding and a new name befitting his new status of abundant provision.

In the face of a national crisis, it seems that Pharaoh saw Joseph as "Mr. Unlimited Source of Supply," or the man with the revelation of God's prosperity principles. Joseph had only spoken the plan and presented the divine principles, but Pharaoh saw him as the full answer to the need.

The divine plan was released by Joseph speaking it, then the Spirit of God produced faith in Pharaoh toward Joseph, as if Joseph already was the source of full supply. **Faith cometh by hearing, and hearing by the word of God** (Rom. 10:17). Joseph released God's Word by boldly declaring God's Plan of Plenty, and Pharaoh believed there would be an abundant supply in the time of famine if God's Word was obeyed.

Speaking God's plan always produces plenty, even in great famine. When men and women release God's Word in the earth the way Joseph did, His Word will not return void. It will accomplish what God desires and it will prosper in the thing [person, place or plan] to which He sends it. (Isa. 55:11 AP.)

You Should Be Called Mr. or Mrs. Plenty

With Christ as your Savior, the principles of God's Word to produce plenty are yours to speak into your famine. In Christ, you are a son of Abraham with the same inheritance Joseph had. Study God's Word and begin now to announce God's promise to provide for you just as He did for Joseph. You will see God's promises fulfilled as you release your faith and begin to speak His plan of plenty into the needs of your life instead of words of failure.

Abundant resources are available to those who obey the divine principles of plenty and who speak of God's faithfulness to provide, regardless of the doom and gloom of the day.

Details of the Plan of Plenty

In this chapter we have seen how Joseph faithfully ruled over all that was given him to oversee. Being a faithful servant who rules over the increase is only a portion of God's Plan of Plenty. His financial principles also require gaining by trading and giving to those who need your supply. Joseph strictly applied each of these divine business principles, which Jesus taught later in Matthew 25 and Luke 19.

In the next chapter we will see how Joseph saved the world from starving by the use of these principles and also made it possible for every person to remain a successful, independent business person without lack in a time of famine. By applying God's Plan of Plenty, Joseph created a healthy world market with an abundance of money to purchase what every individual produced, at a time when there was no other source of money or market in the world. Joseph applied financial principles that God had instructed him to follow. As a result, there was a better cash market during a time of world famine than when the world was producing plenty.

A Prosperous Appearance Can Be an Advantage in Witnessing

It is interesting that Joseph maintained a physical appearance which displayed the prosperity of God on his life. As a young man, he wore the coat of many colors that his father had given him. When he was called to visit the Pharaoh, Scripture states that Joseph shaved and changed his clothes. Joseph knew it was important to make a good first impression with the Egyptian leader he was called to influence.

Some people think it is ridiculous to talk of prosperity and to look like you have plenty. Let me show you from Scripture how a prosperous appearance can be a great advantage for you when witnessing to a world in need. God promises abundant life, and when the world sees you as one who possesses wealth, you are a testimony of God's goodness. As you witness to them of Jesus, they will listen more intently and more often when you appear to possess the wealth of the wealthy God you represent.

Let this scriptural example speak for itself to encourage you in this matter:

> **And after certain days, when Felix came with his wife Drusilla, which was a Jewess, he sent for Paul, and heard him concerning the faith in Christ.**
>
> **And as he reasoned of righteousness, temperance, and judgment to come, Felix trembled, and answered, Go thy way for this time; when I have a convenient season, I will call for thee.**
>
> **He hoped also that money should have been given him of Paul, that he might loose him: wherefore he sent for him the oftener, and communed with him.**
>
> **But after two years Porcius Festus came into Felix' room: and Felix, willing to shew the Jews a pleasure, left Paul bound.**
>
> **Acts 24:24-27**

These scriptures clearly show that Felix the governor kept Paul near him for two full years and talked with him often. His main purpose for talking with Paul was because he hoped Paul would offer him money to set him free. Therefore, he sent for him more often and communed with him. (Acts 24:26.)

For the rich governor to think Paul had so much money that it was worth keeping him around and talking to him for two full years, Paul either had money, or he talked and acted like he did. Take your pick. Either one or both of the factors had to exist.

Paul Preached Prosperity

I believe Paul included in his Gospel message to the governor what he also preached to others. In Romans 8:32 Paul wrote, **He that spared not his own Son, but delivered him up for us all, how shall he not with him also freely give us all things?** In 2 Corinthians 8:9 Paul taught, **For ye know the grace of our Lord Jesus Christ, that, though he was rich, yet for your sakes he became poor, that ye through his poverty might be rich.**

Paul preached of the wealth Christ had provided for us. The governor must have believed that Paul had the great wealth of which he preached. To make that impression, I believe that Paul must have talked and acted like he had the abundance of God in his own life. Let's be scriptural and speak the principles of plenty in Christ Jesus like Paul did!

9

Joseph the Gainer

God revealed to Joseph that the way to survive the approaching famine was to *save* during times of plenty in order to prepare for the times of lack. We are taught of this concept of "storehouse preparation" in both the Old and New Testaments.

One New Testament example is found in the parable of the five wise and five foolish virgins in Matthew 25:1-13. The five foolish women were those who did not plan ahead by having the excess oil they needed in order to burn the lamps long into the dark night. Because they were not prepared and had to return to town to buy more oil for their lamps, they were shut out of the celebration when the bridegroom came. The women who prepared for the coming darkness by taking excess oil for their lamps represent those who have the wisdom to prepare for the return of Jesus by being filled with the Holy Spirit, knowing God's Word, and possessing adequate material wealth for His service.

In the Old Testament, Noah *prepared* for the impending crisis of the flood. When God forewarned him, Noah began to build and store supplies because he believed the Word of God. *What destroyed others established Noah as king of the earth.* On board the ark, he had more in excess in one place than he ever had before. Crisis time is Good News to the righteous, who prepare and do things God's way while holding to the exactness of God's Word.

For over a hundred years, Noah prepared for the coming flood. God told Noah that building an ark was the only way to safety and blessings in the coming crisis. Others who saw what Noah was doing could have repented and prepared for the flood too. Yet only eight persons believed God's Word and obediently prepared. What was destruction to the entire unbelieving majority was ultimate prosperity to those who prepared in obedience to God. They had an abundant storehouse, designed by God himself. They worked for one hundred years to prepare it exactly the way He told them. God did not provide supernatural manna on the ark. *Storehouse preparation is a divine principle.*

Joseph Opened a Savings Account

Joseph believed that *saving for the future* was a divine principle. God had told him to *save* a portion of the grain during the seven years of plenty in order to prepare for the seven years of famine.

Now therefore let Pharaoh look out a man discreet and wise, and set him over the land of Egypt.

Let Pharaoh do this, and let him appoint officers over the land, and take up the fifth part [20 percent] of the land of Egypt in the seven plenteous years.

And let them gather all the food of those good years that come, and *lay up* **corn under the hand of Pharaoh, and let them** *keep* **food in the cities.**

And that food shall be for *store* **to the land against the seven years of famine, which shall be in the land of Egypt; that the land perish not through famine.**

Genesis 41:33-36

In these verses, we see the beginning of God's plan of plenty to prevent lack in famine. Joseph presented a way to prosper by creating a world market to supply everyone's needs. His plan foreshadow's the principles of financial success which Jesus taught in Matthew 25 and Luke 19. Joseph's application of the principles of ruling over what you have been given, gaining by trading, and giving to those in need made it possible for the whole world to survive with plenty of food in Egypt when there wasn't supposed to be any.

Taxes Are God's Idea for Financial Success

As far as we can see in Bible history, no nation or kingdom had ever instituted taxes before Joseph's plan to prosper Egypt. First, Joseph suggested to Pharaoh that he put a wise and discreet man over the business of the land of Egypt. Then Joseph said he should appoint officers (tax collectors) to take up the fifth part (20 percent) of the crops of Egypt in the seven plenteous years. (Gen. 41:34.)

Through Joseph's plan, the initiation of fair taxes was established as part of a divine plan of plenty for the nation. Even a nation cannot succeed by providing services free of charge. It is part of God's plan for a government to levy taxes for the necessary services to its subjects It is also necessary, according to divine plan, for a government to apply the rest of the formula necessary for financial success, which is: To rule over what is given to it by controlling spending while offering charitable services to those with legitimate needs. Joseph introduced and applied all of these principles during this time of crisis in Egypt.

God's Plan of Plenty Reaches Pharaoh

A message of doom and gloom and doing without did not motivate a picky, pagan king. The message of doom does not win the attention of many people today, either. A plan of plenty to prosper during a time of famine did inspire Pharaoh to believe God's Word. People still need to hear that God's plan is to prosper them, not to harm them.

Pharaoh liked the idea of preparing for the future by collecting taxes. He liked the Plan of Plenty, the well-groomed man who presented the plan, and the God whom the man with divine truth represented.

Joseph Begins the Plan of Plenty

And Joseph was thirty years old when he stood before Pharaoh king of Egypt. And Joseph went out from the presence of Pharaoh, and went throughout all the land of Egypt.

And in the seven plenteous years the earth brought forth by handfuls.

And he gathered up all the food of the seven years, which were in the land of Egypt, and *laid up* the food in the cities: the food of the field, which was round about every city, laid he up in the same.

And Joseph gathered corn as the sand of the sea, very much, until he left numbering; for it was without number.

Genesis 41:46-49

In the first phase of Joseph's plan of plenty, he *gathered and stored* what would be lacking after the seven years of plenty were completed. He stored it in every city. *He was not storing the food to give it away.* It was not part of the divine principle to give it *all* away. You will see through Joseph's plan why the divine principle is to sell for profit, even when there is a need. If you do not sell for profit, you won't have the resources to meet needs in the future.

There must be a margin of profit in order for there to be a continual, unlimited source of meeting needs. This is a divine principle. God wants His people to be a source of unlimited supply. The divine principle is to *gain by trading, then give out of the increase.* Do not give your products away; *give from the profits of selling your products.*

Saving, Storehousing and Selling Products

And the seven years of dearth began to come, according as Joseph had said: and the dearth was in all lands; but in all the land of Egypt there was bread.

And when all the land of Egypt was famished, the people cried to Pharaoh for bread: and Pharaoh said unto all the Egyptians, Go unto Joseph; what he saith to you, do.

And the famine was over all the face of the earth: and Joseph opened all the *storehouses*, and *sold* unto the Egyptians; and the famine waxed sore in the land of Egypt.

And all countries came into Egypt to Joseph for *to buy* corn; because that the famine was so sore in all lands.

Genesis 41:54-57

In the above verses, we have seen the principles of Matthew 25:14 and Luke 19:12 applied by Joseph. He *saved, stored* and *prepared* products the world needed. Then he *sold* to his own countrymen and then to all the world.

The whole world would have perished if Joseph had given away all he had stored because there was great need. He could not have continued to be the source of continual supply by giving away more than he received.

His *temptation* to give it all away must have been great when he saw the needs of the people. But he would have violated a divine financial principle, and he would have failed to meet the needs of people once his source of supply was gone.

The sign on his locked storehouse door would read:

CLOSED BECAUSE OF BANKRUPTCY

I regret to announce that this storehouse of supply has depleted its resources;
it was all out-go with no in-flow.
I violated the divine principle of not gaining with giving!
I can't give to you even though I want to.
I disobeyed God by not gaining in business;
therefore, I have failed you, for which I am sorry.

If Joseph had violated the divine principle of supply by not selling for profit and by giving it all away, he would have been the reason that the world *perished*. God had given him the plan to prosper and not fail. God has given us the same plan to provide a source of supply for our lives.

By being obedient to God's plan, Joseph was the *answer* to a world threatened by famine, and his obedience saved the people and caused them to *thrive* in a time of lack. There is no lack when you consistently do things God's way. **The Lord is my shepherd, I shall not be in want** (Ps. 23:1 NIV). By obeying God's Word and voice you can prevent lack in your world.

Joseph Continued to Sell and Gather Wealth for Egypt

Joseph continued to sell the abundant supply of corn which he had wisely stored in Egypt. He sold to the Egyptians and to all the countries of the world. Soon, all the *money* in Egypt and in all the land of Canaan was safely *stored* in Pharaoh's rich treasury. His vast imperial treasury vaults were laden with all the gold of Egypt. **And Joseph gathered up all the *money* that was found in the land of Egypt, and in the land of Canaan, for the corn which they bought: and Joseph brought the money into Pharaoh's house** (Gen. 47:14).

Joseph continued to gain, regardless of the world condition, because he was obeying the plan from God. Soon all the money of Egypt and Canaan was in the hands of Joseph. **And when money failed in the land of Egypt, and in the land of Canaan, all the Egyptians came unto Joseph, and said, *Give us* bread: for why should we die in thy presence? for the money faileth** (Gen. 47:15).

Even when the people came and asked him to give to them, *Joseph held to the principle of gaining by trading.* He was not dealing with destitute people who did not have the resources to pay for food. They had cattle, livestock and land. Joseph did not let his heart get in the way here. He still held to the divine principle of not giving it all away. He continued to rule over the increase for God and gained by trading.

Joseph was the *only* person in all the world who was being tough enough to obey the divine principles of guaranteed supply by selling what was needed for a profit and giving a percentage of the increase. Had he not obeyed these principles, he would not have had what the people of the world needed. He was the *only hope* for the world to be fed. If he had violated the principle that God established in order to maintain a continual supply, he would have betrayed the world.

People may have thought he was betraying them by selling them corn instead of just giving it to them. They had pleaded for mercy and they could have said, "You are a charlatan who has betrayed the God you say you serve by charging for what was shown to you supernaturally. We don't think you should put a price on the knowledge God has given to you. Give to us. It's not right to make us pay. Give to us!"

Joseph was in a hard position, and it would have been easy to give in to sentiment. But he held to divine principles so that the world could survive. Through his unwavering obedience to the principles of unlimited supply, they were fed. Joseph did this by faith, not feelings.

When the world asked him to give them bread, he by faith held to the divine plan and *sold* to them instead. There would have been no well of plenty in the future for mankind if he had not sold. If he had given it all away, the well would have been dry forever!

For the good of all, Joseph continued to *sell*, even though there was no more money. He answered those who asked for bread but whose money was gone,

Give [trade] your cattle; and I will give you for your cattle, if money fail.

And they brought their cattle unto Joseph: and Joseph gave them bread in exchange for horses, and for the flocks, and for the cattle of the herds, and for the asses: and he fed them with bread for all their cattle for that year.

Genesis 47:16,17

Joseph Gains the Labor Force and the Land of Egypt

In one year Joseph had all the money and all the cattle in the land. He had everything but the land and homes of the people of Egypt. Then they came to him and asked him to *buy* their land and let them work for him, so they would not starve in the great and terrible drought over all the earth. They believed he could keep them from starving.

It must have been easy to have confidence in Joseph. The people knew he was a person who *never lost* in the situations of life and who treated them fairly. They respected him for not allowing himself or Pharaoh to be cheated, depleted or defeated. They trusted that he had an unlimited supply and that he would deal fairly with them.

They knew he would not cheat them. He had charged them in hard situations of the past, which they knew was difficult for him to do. Now they had confidence that they could trust a man like this and never have to worry about perishing from hunger or financial crisis. Joseph was a man who applied divine principles as he ruled over his master's goods and gained by trading in order to give from the increase. Therefore, when their supplies ran out, the people offered to work for him in exchange for food.

When that year was ended, they came unto him the second year, and said unto him, We will not hide it from my lord, how that our money is spent; my lord also hath our herds of cattle; there is not aught left in the sight of my lord, but our bodies, and our lands:

Wherefore shall we die before thine eyes, both we
and our land? *buy us* and our land for bread, and we
and our land will be servants unto Pharaoh: and give us
seed, that we may live, and not die, that the land be not
desolate.

And Joseph bought all the land of Egypt for
Pharaoh; for the Egyptians sold every man his field,
because the famine prevailed over them so the land
became Pharaoh's.

And as for the people, he removed them to cities
from one end of the borders of Egypt even to the other
end thereof.

Genesis 47:18-21

Independent Businessmen

The people had no money because Joseph already had
all the money. When he bought their land and services, he
gave them seed to sow in the land (v. 23) and told them to
once again give a fifth of the increase to Pharaoh and keep
four parts for future seed and food (v. 24). Joseph made it
possible for every person to be their own independent
business person. Each could be as small or as large in
business as they had the energy and incentive to be.

For those who joined the program, he strategically
moved them to where they would be the most productive.
They also had a central city market for the sale of the
products they produced and for Pharaoh's storage for
future world market needs.

They now had the opportunity to apply the same divine
principles that Joseph had applied by ruling over what had
been given to them, gaining by trading and giving from
their increase.

Priests' Privileges

Only the land of the priests bought he not; for the
priests had a portion assigned them of Pharaoh, and did

eat their portion which Pharaoh gave them: wherefore they sold not their lands.

Genesis 47:22

From the increase, Joseph provided a charity benefit plan for the priests in the land. Pharaoh granted them abundant, free provisions of food and allowed them to keep their land. The priests were tax exempt. Joseph gave the priests special privileges in order to let them be free to serve the Lord.

This financial plan for priests was from God, coming through Joseph. It was the principle of giving that is a part of God's Plan of Plenty for the economic prosperity of mankind. If you do not give for the work of the Lord, you will not fully prosper the way God intends for you to prosper.

We will cover more of the giving part of Joseph's plan of prosperity in chapter 10. But now, let's continue to study his plan to gain by trading which he also established for every man in Egypt who wanted to participate. Joseph taught the people of Egypt to rule over, gain and give from the increase—even in great drought!

Joseph's Prosperity Plan for Everyone in Egypt

Although Joseph seemed to be a very hard man in business matters, he was interested in more than just winning for himself. He wanted God's plan to be followed. He wanted everyone to win.

He was interested in Pharaoh prospering. He saw to it that Potiphar and the ruler of the king's prison prospered. He saw to it that the prison prospered when he was put in charge of it. He was even concerned why the chief butler and chief baker were not happy in prison, and he did what he could to encourage them. Then, in the middle of a worldwide famine, we see Joseph is interested in every man in Egypt prospering more than they ever had on their own.

Joseph was true to the principles of God's Plan of Plenty. His obedience caused him to win in business and in all of life. His love for people and his desire for them to prosper was the same as God's. He enjoyed giving, which is the charity principle of God's Plan of Plenty.

Joseph did more than just apply what seemed to be the hard-hearted business principle of selling for gain. He also gave from his increase and shared with others the knowledge of how to succeed. He wanted everyone else to apply the same principles so everyone could win.

Because of the desperate needs of the people, it would have been so easy for him to give it all away. But he continued to practice the principles of ruling, gaining and giving and began to teach each man in Egypt the following threefold principles of God's Plan of Plenty that had caused him to succeed:

> **Then Joseph said unto the people, Behold, I have bought you this day and your land for Pharaoh: lo, here is seed for you, and ye shall sow the land.**
>
> **And it shall come to pass in the increase, that ye shall give the fifth part [20 percent] unto Pharaoh, and four parts [80 percent] shall be your own, for seed of the field, and for your food, and for them of your households, and for food for your little ones.**
>
> **And they said, Thou [Joseph] hast saved our lives: let us find grace in the sight of my lord, and we will be Pharaoh's servants.**
>
> **Genesis 47:23-25**

A Review of Joseph's Agreement With the People

The people were grateful because they were not agreeing to slavery. They were entering into a contractual agreement with the most successful financial genius the world had ever known, who was running the wealthiest kingdom the world had ever known. Rich archeological discoveries have since proven the great wealth of this time in Egypt.

Joseph served God and was genuinely interested in all people being successful and without lack. He had bought their land at their request and agreed to accept their labor in exchange for the provisions they needed. He had bought their land, he had not confiscated it, nor taken them over as slaves. They loved his deal and appeared to be honored at the privilege of this opportunity to work for him.

With the money Joseph gave them for their land and the seed he had given them to sow the land, they had an opportunity to recover from the disaster of the famine. With the money and contractual work for a man known for divine fairness, they were given much more than they had before the famine. They were given security to keep them wealthy, backed by the riches of Egypt. Plus, they were given financial instructions on how to be successful like Joseph was. Even his finance seminar was free to them.

Joseph moved them to central cities, gave them seed and taught them profit-sharing. He gave them financial training on what to do with the great profits they were sure to make:

• Give 20 percent (1/5) of their increase to their government.

• Keep 80 percent (4/5) for themselves to reinvest and use for themselves.

For their 20 percent Joseph furnished the land, the seeds, the market, arranged to collect for goods sold and gave them their share. They didn't have to worry about where to plant, how to start, where to sell, when to pay or be concerned about being paid by bad checks. The plan was hassle-free for everyone involved! They didn't even have to worry about negotiating international prices.

Their wages for only producing the product were the unusually high (and not even requested) wage of 80 percent of the sale! That's right, 80 percent! They didn't even demand it; Joseph just gave it to them.

Many successful business principles can be gleaned from this illustration. For example, profits don't have to be high when increasing and maintaining are consistent. We also see that the key to consistent quality-controlled products is to pay trained labor well, as if they were independent business people working by the incentive of high profits for quality production. This way, each man can be as rich as he wants to be. He can have as many people work for him as he wants. When production or quality is poor, there is no pay; when it is high and good, the pay is astronomical.

Biblical Economic Principles

Some of Joseph's teachings on financial management begin in Genesis 41:24. It is essential to *manage* the "take home" portion of our income and save some for reinvestment if we want to see God's Plan of Plenty operate in our lives. This is a biblical principle of finance necessary for success.

Part of your income must be appropriated for "seed" to produce your product the next year. Part of your profit must be for food and for those of your household, which includes salaries and benefits for those who work for you. Part of the portion you keep is for food for your children.

It is important to budget the 80 percent portion that you keep for your own expenses. Some is for savings, some is for bills and some is for your family's provisions. This is money for the full care of you, your family, your personal expenses, automobiles, home, insurance, God's tithe, giving to the poor, special offerings, permanent savings, investments, entertainment, vacations, recreation, educational expenses, including campmeetings and believers' conventions.

The Egyptians responded to Joseph's financial plan with gratitude for being a part of God's financial plan of abundance in the midst of the worst world famine in the history of man. They eagerly submitted to Joseph's plan, recognizing his directions as sound teaching. They excitedly said in grateful accord, "You [Joseph] have saved our lives!" (v. 25).

Joseph Foreshadowed the Teaching of Matthew 25

Joseph fully understood and applied the threefold principles of ruling, gaining and giving found in Matthew 25:14-30. He even taught these principles to the citizens of Egypt and set each man up in business for himself to apply the principles.

He taught them to expect a high profit for producing quality products and rendering excellent services. Jesus clearly taught this same principle in Matthew 25:14-30 and Luke 19:11-27. It is scriptural for a faithful servant of God to gain great profits by trading and to maintain control over the gain by *managing* the profits in order to continue increasing wealth for the Lord's work.

Joseph taught these principles too. He had heard from God. These divine principles are found throughout God's Word. Through the ages, God has offered these principles for every individual to apply. The Lord is unchanging. If you gain by trading your seed and ask Him where to give the increase, He will still say, "Well done, good and faithful servant!"

Joseph Bought the World

Joseph acquired all the money, all the land, all the livestock and the entire labor force in Egypt. A current example of a nation who is gaining by trading the way Joseph did is found in how Japan has prospered by selling its products to America. Whether they are aware of it or not, Japanese business people have applied the principles of being the head by being faithful over little and gaining an increase through marketing their product.

Sony, a Japanese-owned company, paid 3.4 billion dollars for Columbia Pictures. Twenty-one months earlier, a Japanese corporation purchased CBS Records for 2 billion dollars. Since then, billions of cash dollars have been paid by the Japanese in purchasing prime U.S. real estate and major U.S. companies.

From Rubble to Riches

The utter devastation and poverty of Japan during World War II almost annihilated the country. The charitable assistance of America, headed by General Douglas MacArthur, saved Japan from hopelessness. The Japanese could have continued to receive America's assistance and remained dependent upon the goodness of our Christian charity, but they did not.

They could have decided, "I will show my appreciation to America's charity by giving my goods and services to the kind Americans." They could have felt obliged to do good deeds and offer free gifts to the Americans forever. Had the Japanese done this, they would have been a constant and permanent cost to America. Dependent Japan would have become a never-ending liability. Eventually our supply of charitable support would have been depleted.

Instead of receiving free handouts, the Japanese began to sell goods and services to America, their source of charitable aid. This was not to repay charity but to end the need of being a recipient of charity. If they had felt that they could not have charged us because we had been so good to them, they would never have had the means to become independent.

However, the Japanese began to apply the Principle of Gaining by Trading and selling goods as a planned profit to meet a market's need or a market's "want." As a result they acquired their financial independence and were able to remove themselves from the dependency of charity.

One way they began was by making tin toys to sell to the children of America. They collected what appeared to be "clutter and trash" from their war-torn and littered land. The source of their beautiful tin toys, so eagerly purchased by the charitable and forgiving Americans, was what the American G.I. had cluttered their land with—the plain, old ugly, seemingly worthless, American G.I. beer can. What most see as clutter, the Japanese began to see as glitter.

They could have said, "We don't have the equipment or resources to make a product the Americans would want to buy." When they decided to gain regardless and did not yield to negatives, the spiritual law of "ingenuity" produced a way. They took the cans from the heap of clutter, turned them inside out and shaped them into irresistible toys.

What brought joy to American kids by buying what they wanted gave joy to Japanese kids by supplying what they needed. Eventually, through gaining by trading, they were also able to buy what they "wanted." This was possible by following a *definite plan for making profit* through marketing goods and services.

The end result of this scriptural Principle of Gaining by Trading to a market has made it possible for the Japanese to purchase what they want of American business, entertainment and resources. Their selling did not stop with the sale of toys to the American kids. They have continued to sell "toys" to the same generation of American "kids" through the years. Their cars, motorbikes, electronic gadgets, TV's, VCR's, and computers are just "bigger toys for bigger boys."

Japan has profited through a biblical plan of marketing an unlimited supply of products that the world wants. They were faithful over little, and now they are masters over much.

America needs to continue to give to countries who need our help, but we must *balance our charity* with the second great biblical principle of financial success of *gaining by trading*. The Japanese have been diligent to apply this principle of increase. It's beginning to appear that the Japanese could buy the world like Joseph did! Perhaps they will become our landlords, if we don't balance our charity with selling and managing.

The main need the entire world has is Jesus, but money is needed to carry the Good News that His prosperity is for all who will accept Him as their Savior. Christian business people can send full-time preachers when they aren't called to go themselves. The money to do that must come from Christians who know how to market their goods and services for a profit.

The full-time ministers and missionaries must also expect profits from what they do, for it was Jesus himself who taught the seventy missionaries to accept what was offered to them saying, **...for the labourer** [the full-time minister of the Gospel] **is worthy of his hire** [his pay for spiritual duties performed] (Luke 10:7). The principle of increase applies to full-time ministers also.

The threefold principles of ruling, gaining and giving were active in the life of Joseph. (Gen. 45:17-27.) Joseph gained the entire world for the nation of Egypt by being obedient to God's Plan of Plenty! Obeying these principles will bring God's best into your life and put you in the position of being the head and not the tail, just like Joseph.

10
Joseph the Giver

Because Joseph knew how to manage and rule over finances, he was given an honored position over the wealth of Egypt. The authority he was granted made it possible for him to give God's people the best even in a famine.

At the insistence of Pharaoh, Joseph sent fleets of wagons and chariots to the land of Canaan to bring the blessed family of God, Israel, to the best the world had.

> Haste ye, and go up to my father, and say unto him, Thus saith thy son Joseph, God hath made me lord of all Egypt: come down unto me, tarry not:
>
> And thou shalt dwell in the land of Goshen, and thou shalt be near unto me, thou, and thy children, and thy children's children, and thy flocks, and thy herds, and all that thou hast:
>
> And there will I nourish thee; for yet there are five years of famine; lest thou, and thy household, and all that thou hast, come to poverty.
>
> Genesis 45:9-11

Even Pharaoh Commands the Best for God's People

And *Pharaoh said* unto Joseph, Say unto thy brethren, This do ye; lade your beasts, and go, get you unto the land of Canaan;

And take your father and your households, and come unto me: and *I will give you the good of the land of Egypt,* and ye shall eat the fat of the land.

Now thou art commanded, this do ye; take you wagons out of the land of Egypt for your little ones, and for your wives, and bring your father, and come.

Also regard not your stuff; for the good of all the land of Egypt is yours.

And the children of Israel did so: and Joseph gave them wagons, according to the commandment of Pharaoh, and gave them provision for the way.

To all of them he gave each man changes of raiment; but to Benjamin he gave three hundred pieces of silver, and five changes of raiment.

And to his father he sent after this manner; ten asses laden with the good things of Egypt, and ten she asses laden with corn and bread and meat for his father by the way.

So he sent his brethren away, and they departed: and he said unto them, See that ye fall not out by the way.

And they went up out of Egypt, and came into the land of Canaan unto Jacob their father,

And told him, saying, Joseph is yet alive, and he is governor over all the land of Egypt. And Jacob's heart fainted, for he believed them not.

And they told him all the words of Joseph, which he had said unto them: and when he saw the wagons which Joseph had sent to carry him, the spirit of Jacob their father revived.

Genesis 45:17-27

Pharaoh gave Joseph authority that enabled him to give the best to the household of Jacob. Israel, God's chosen people who were to carry His Word throughout the earth, was nourished and prospered because Joseph, the ruler, gainer and giver, was obedient to the divine laws of financial success.

And *Pharaoh spake* unto Joseph, saying, Thy father and thy brethren are come unto thee:

The land of Egypt is before thee; *in the best of the land make thy father and brethren* to dwell; in the land of Goshen let them dwell: and if thou knowest any men of activity among them, then make them rulers over my cattle.

And Joseph brought in Jacob his father, and set him before Pharaoh: and Jacob blessed Pharaoh.

And Pharaoh said unto Jacob, How old art thou?

And Jacob said unto Pharaoh, The days of the years of my pilgrimage are an hundred and thirty years: few and evil have the days of the years of my life been, and have not attained unto the days of the years of the life of my fathers in the days of their pilgrimage.

And Jacob blessed Pharaoh, and went out from before Pharaoh.

And Joseph placed his father and his brethren, and gave them a possession in the land of Egypt, IN THE BEST OF THE LAND [my emphasis], in the land of Rameses, as Pharaoh had commanded.

And Joseph nourished his father, and his brethren, and all his father's household, with bread, according to their families.

Genesis 47:5-12

God's People Are Honored by Pagan Leaders

Details of all Joseph gave to God's people are found in chapters 42 through 50 of Genesis. Joseph's family (about 70 people at the time) were highly honored in Egypt. When Jacob died seventeen years after coming to the flourishing land of Goshen, even all the leaders of Egypt went with Joseph to bury his father. The burial was in Mamre, a 600-mile trip, and there were only camels and horse-drawn chariots in which to travel. The only routes were over the dusty roads of the Middle East deserts, yet Pharaoh commanded his own servants to make the journey with Joseph.

And Pharaoh said, Go up, and bury thy father, according as he made thee swear.

And Joseph went up to bury his father: and with him went up all the servants of Pharaoh, the elders of his house, and all the elders of the land of Egypt,

And all the house of Joseph, and his brethren, and his father's house: only their little ones, and their flocks, and their herds, they left in the land of Goshen.

And there went up with him both chariots and horsemen: and it was a very great company.

And they came to the threshingfloor of Atad, which is beyond Jordan, and there they mourned with a great and very sore lamentation: and he made a mourning for his father seven days.

And when the inhabitants of the land, the Canaanites, saw the mourning in the floor of Atad, they said, This is a grievous mourning to the Egyptians: wherefore the name of it was called Abel-mizraim, which is beyond Jordan.

Genesis 50:6-11

The word *Abel-mizraim* means "all of Egypt mourns."

The Magnitude of the Honor

It was truly a great honor for all of the royal and elite leaders of Egypt to mourn the loss of Joseph's father, Jacob. Hebrews were supposed to be culturally restricted and subordinated in Egypt as slaves. The cultural prejudice was so great that Egyptians considered eating with Hebrews detestable. This cultural restriction was evident when Joseph invited his brothers to his palatial Egyptian home before revealing to them that he was their brother. At the noon meal, because his brothers still thought Joseph was an Egyptian, he ate at a separate table from them.

And Joseph made haste; for his bowels did yearn upon his brother: and he sought where to weep; and he entered into his chamber, and wept there.

> And he washed his face, and went out, and
> refrained himself, and said, Set on bread.
>
> And they set on for him by himself, and for them
> by themselves, and for the Egyptians, which did eat
> with him, by themselves: because the Egyptians might
> not eat bread with the Hebrews; for that is an
> abomination unto the Egyptians.
>
> **Genesis 43:30-32**

In spite of previous differences with the Hebrews, all of
Egypt mourned with the same grief Joseph had at the loss
of his father. The Egyptians cared for Joseph and his people
because Joseph had cared for them with the same care he
had for God's people. And God had given him the resources
to administer that care.

Joseph had the resources to care for others because he
obeyed the divine laws which guaranteed provision to
meet the needs of others. As a result of his obedience, God
made him the head! The whole world honored him, even at
the death of his Hebrew father, which by Egyptian cultural
tradition should have been an abomination!

The ultimate promise of Deuteronomy 28:1-14 is, *God
will make you the head and not the tail, above only and not
beneath.* Because Joseph was obedient to divine law, Joseph
and God's people were honored by the world. The
Egyptians saw and benefited from the fruit of obedience to
God's plan in the life of Joseph.

God's people became the head and not the tail in pagan
and worldly Egypt. Diligence to divine law promises
adoration—not abomination!

You Have Joseph's Right in Christ

**If you belong to Christ, then you are Abraham's seed,
and heirs according to the promise** (Gal. 3:29 NIV). As a
Christian, you have the same right that Joseph had to be the
head, not the tail, and prosper in all you do. Diligence to

God's divine law of grace is the key to your prosperity and headship.

We can learn how to apply these principles in our lives by observing the life of Joseph. Everywhere he went, Joseph gave of himself for God. Without compromising, Joseph held to the laws that guarantee success. He was a ruler, a gainer and a giver. He was a diligent witness of God's power and provision in word and deed before family, friends, strangers, peasants and kings. He was faithful to God in every situation.

He was a mature heir of the kingdom and, like Abraham, he served God. To receive our inheritance we must mature in the knowledge of God's promises for us and administrate His Word to the needs of the dying world which Christ came to save.

We are heirs to the promise God made to Abraham. Galatians 4:1 explains that as long as the heir is a child, he is no different from a slave, even though he owns the whole estate. A mature heir understands his inheritance. When you know and exercise your rights as Joseph did, you will receive the provision God has granted to you as His heir. Here is the reassurance of your inheritance:

> So also, when we were children, we were in slavery under the basic principles of the world. But when the time had fully come, God sent his Son, born of a woman, born under law, to redeem those under law, that we might receive the *full rights of sons* [emphasis mine]. Because you are sons, God sent the Spirit of his Son into our hearts, the Spirit who calls out, "Abba, Father." So you are no longer a slave but a son; and since you are a son, God has made you also an heir.
> **Galatians 4:3-7** NIV

Paul asks Christians in the fourth chapter of Galatians, "Now that you know God—or rather are known by God—how is it that you are turning back to those weak and miserable principles that keep you in bondage?"

The principles of this world wanted to keep Joseph in bondage, but he stood for what was right according to the word God had given him. He knew that obedience was better than sacrifice. Joseph received his inheritance as a seed of Abraham because he was obedient to God's plan for his life.

As you are faithful to obey God's Word and show yourself as a mature heir of Abraham's blessing, you will receive full rights to the inheritance of God's promises as Joseph did.

Ruling, gaining, giving and living right are your keys to God's full heritage benefits. The thief comes to steal, kill and destroy, but Jesus came that we might have life, and have it more abundantly. (John 10:10.) His Word is guaranteed by His own blood and His promise is abundant life. As heir to this promise, may we walk in the fullness of His power!

11
It's Time to Receive
Your Inheritance

It's time to receive God's provision so that people will be cared for and God will be glorified. To receive what God has prepared for you, start with the principles of ruling, gaining and giving in obedience to God's Word. Start where you are.

You may feel like you don't have anything to rule over, but you can begin by ruling over the knowledge of His truth concerning His desire to bless you. When doubt begins to rob you of the promise of His blessing, apply the principles of ruling, gaining and giving to your own faith. Rebuke doubt and unbelief. Gain more faith by studying God's Word and share your faith with someone else by believing with them for the needs in their life.

Joseph had nothing to work with but these principles in most of the situations that life presented to him. He diligently applied the threefold principles of ruling, gaining and giving in his father's house, Potiphar's palatial home, the king's executive prison, appearing before Pharaoh, dealing with the starving Egyptians, selling to the world and with his own needy brothers.

Abraham's Successful Heirs Began
Only With the Principles

Both Jacob and Joseph, direct heirs of Abraham, were cut off from the material wealth of their heritage.

Nevertheless, they amassed great fortunes and were prosperous in all they did.

The story of Jacob's life is found in Genesis 27-35. Jacob *bought* his brother's birthright for a bowl of soup. When Esau realized that he had given up the blessing that was granted to the firstborn son, he wanted to kill Jacob. In fear for his life, Jacob ran from Esau and was separated from the material heritage of his grandfather, Abraham, for twenty years.

God spoke to Jacob in a dream and promised to bless him. When he was cut off from his family, friends and wealthy inheritance, Jacob made a commitment to give God the tithe of all he believed God would give to him. He began to apply the principles that his grandfather, Abraham, first established—before he even had a job or material possessions to give. As a result, Jacob acquired great wealth while he was in exile and then received the full material heritage of his father, Isaac, when he returned home. He began giving from his gain, even before his increase came:

> **And Jacob vowed a vow, saying, If God will be with me, and will keep me in this way that I go, and will give me bread to eat, and raiment to put on,**
>
> **So that I come again to my father's house in peace, then the Lord be my God:**
>
> **And this stone, which I have set for a pillar, shall be God's house: and of all that thou shalt give me I will surely give the tenth unto thee.**
>
> **Genesis 28:20-22**

Although he had nothing to begin with except principles, Jacob pledged to give God ten percent of his income. With only a stone for a pillow, Jacob applied the principles which had produced prosperity for Abraham. Jacob knew God had promised to bless him. In this obscure place of desert isolation, he committed to give to God a tenth of all he was about to receive.

Jacob was totally cut off from the benefits of his material heritage when he vowed to give God the tithe. He didn't have a job to rule over with his management skills. He didn't have seed with which to gain an increase. He didn't have money with which to tithe. He didn't know *how* God was going to bless him, but *he had God's Word as a promise* and the principles of faith that his grandfather, Abraham, had used.

Jacob Applies Principles of Righteousness

Jacob began by seeking the will of God for his life, then he acted on the word God gave him. Jacob did what was right in the eyes of God even when others treated him unfairly. For twenty years he worked for Laban, his uncle and father-in-law, who repeatedly cheated Jacob by changing his wages ten times. Yet Jacob was faithful to continue working for his uncle with all of his strength. Because Jacob remained righteous in the eyes of God, the Lord blessed his work and didn't let anything or anyone harm him. (Gen. 31:6,7.)

Jacob **increased exceedingly, and had much cattle, and maidservants, and menservants, and camels, and asses** (Gen. 30:43) because God was with him. Laban's sons began to complain because Jacob had gained all the wealth that had belonged to their father.

Laban, Jacob's unrighteous father-in-law who was once rich, was stripped of his royal wealth because of his sinful acts against righteous Jacob. Jacob was honest, and Laban was not. Jacob sought God, but Laban's household was filled with images of false gods.

Jacob came to work for Laban empty-handed, with only divine principles to apply to his acts of willing service. Laban tried to cheat Jacob every way imaginable during the twenty years Jacob served him. Still, God took wealth away from Laban and gave it to Jacob. (Gen. 31:9.) God prospered

Jacob's livestock business, which his sons ran for him while he worked for Laban. (Gen. 30:35,36,40.)

Then God told Jacob it was time to return to the land of his father and receive his inheritance for the honest work he had given, but Laban tried to stop him from leaving. God met Laban in a dream and told him not to try to stop Jacob. In defense of the grievous acts that were made against him, Jacob said to Laban:

> This twenty years have I been with thee; thy ewes and thy she goats have not cast their young, and the rams of thy flock have I not eaten.
>
> That which was torn of beasts I brought not unto thee; I bare the loss of it; of my hand didst thou require it, whether stolen by day, or stolen by night.
>
> Thus I was; in the day the drought consumed me, and the frost by night; and my sleep departed from mine eyes.
>
> Thus have I been twenty years in thy house; I served thee fourteen years for thy two daughters, and six years for thy cattle: and thou hast changed my wages ten times.
>
> Except the God of my father, the God of Abraham, and the fear of Isaac, had been with me, surely thou hadst sent me away now empty. God hath seen mine affliction and the labour of my hands, and rebuked thee yesternight.
>
> Genesis 31:38-42

Laban responded by asking to make a covenant of peace with Jacob.

> These daughters are my daughters, and these children are my children, and these cattle are my cattle, and all that thou seest is mine: and what can I do this day unto these my daughters, or unto their children which they have born?
>
> Now therefore come thou, let us make a covenant, I and thou; and let it be for a witness between me and thee.
>
> Genesis 31:43,44

Jacob practiced the principles of honest trading for gain and faithful giving of his service to God's work that his grandfather Abraham had followed. The dishonest Laban stood stripped of his great wealth by a man who traded fairly with him and who gave to God from his increase. And yet, Laban wanted to part in peace with the man who took all he had by fair trade practices.

God's promises were fulfilled in the life of Jacob, who applied biblical principles of honest trade with consistent giving. *Jacob gave his time when he didn't have money to give, and he remained faithful even when treated unfairly.* Laban feared Jacob, knowing that God was with him, so he wanted to remain at peace with his son-in-law.

Proverbs 16:7 says, **When a man's ways please the Lord, he maketh even his enemies to be a peace with him.** When you are obedient to His Word, God promises in Deuteronomy 28:7-10 to bless the work of your hands, your storehouse and to defeat your enemies. He will establish you as His holy people if you walk in His ways. Both of these promises were fulfilled in Jacob's life when Laban stood before him asking for a covenant of peace. As a believer in Christ, these promises are also for you.

Jacob *gained* all Laban had by applying righteous principles. I believe if Laban had applied the *principles of righteousness* they would have both been wealthy when they parted. God warned Laban in a dream, **Take heed that thou speak not to Jacob either good or bad** (Gen. 31:24). After Laban heard and believed the Word of God, he happily initiated a covenant of peace with the man who had spoiled his vast wealth by *righteous trading* and *consistent giving.* Jacob had only taken what they had agreed was fair wages. Laban could not stand against the honesty, integrity and truth that Jacob's life represented.

A Gradual Transfer to the Just

The transfer of wicked Laban's wealth to Jacob did not come by a single divine act of God. The transfer came as Jacob consistently applied the principles of ruling, gaining, giving and living righteously. These are the guaranteed principles of consistent financial success which insure the wealth to the just. God promises victory to all who will trust His Word and obey His law.

The Reward Will Come

It took twenty years for both Jacob and Joseph to receive their full inheritance. Regardless of the challenges facing them, they prospered steadily and remained faithful to believe the promise God had given them concerning their future. After twenty years of hiding from Esau, Jacob was instructed by God to return home to the land of Abraham. Although he was empty-handed when he left this land of his rich heritage, he returned with vast numbers of cattle, sheep, goats, donkeys, camels, servants, a family of valiant sons and vast, accumulated wealth. He, who made vows of tithing when he had no substance for living, returned a triumphant princely sultan of wealth. He returned as the head and not the tail, as God's divine principles promised.

Joseph and Jacob had only principles to apply. But in twenty years of applying the principles of ruling, gaining and giving they both had the wealth of Abraham fully in their possession. This was not by inheriting Abraham's money or possessions; they had been cut off from his wealth. These heirs of Abraham inherited the *principles of faith*. Their wealth was guaranteed when they applied the principles to whatever task was before them.

Obedience to God puts you in a "right standing" relationship with Him. We have been told to trust in Jesus Christ for our right to be heirs to the promises of Abraham. Through seeking the kingdom of God and His righteousness we are promised that *all* things will be added unto us. When Jesus taught this in Matthew 6:24-33, He was referring to everything we need in life, from food to beautiful garments. He compared God's provision to the beauty of the lilies of the field and said that even Solomon in all his glory didn't compare to what God had for those who would seek Him.

If you will live the way you saw Jesus live, letting Him live through you, you will live the lifestyle of righteousness that we have just examined in Abraham, Joseph and Jacob. In Christ, you have an eternal right to operate the principles they used and benefit from the promises they received. Have you been cut off from the inheritance that is yours through Christ? If so, begin now to apply these principles, and your inheritance will be restored to you according to God's promise to Abraham.

Faithfulness is not an overnight test. Both Jacob and Joseph diligently applied the principles for twenty years before they received their full inheritance. Faithfulness took them through challenging situations and then into the full promises of God. They believed God even when everything looked impossible. They acted righteously (did the right thing) even when others treated them wrongly.

God is no respecter of persons. I believe that the material wealth promised and given to Abraham, Jacob and Joseph will be the same for any believer in Christ who righteously applies these same principles.

More Than Wealth

God's blessings are eternal and affect eternity. When Jacob applied the principles of ruling, gaining and giving, God gave more than wealth to Jacob. God gave all of humanity the full blessing of His Plan for Flowing Wealth for mankind through Jacob's obedience.

Through Jacob's faithful walk with God and his willingness to submit to God's plan for his life, the nation of Israel came forth from his loins. One by one, twelve valiant sons were born to Jacob and God's plan for the twelve tribes of Israel began to appear in the world.

Jacob was one, then he was twelve, and then he was a nation called Israel. And through the Jewish lineage of the family of Israel, the world was given Jesus—all He was, all He is, and all He will ever be. Jesus chose His disciples from the children of Israel, through whom He spread the Good News of His adoption plan for the Gentiles to join the family of God.

Between the time of Jacob and Jesus, the world was given the wealth of knowing both the presence, the power and the character of Father God as seen in the covenants God made with the children of Israel. Descendants of Israel faithfully recorded the Old and New Testaments, with the history of Adam and Eve, the garden of Eden and the commandments given to Moses. From Israel we have David, Solomon, the prophets, and the Virgin Mary.

The nation of Israel brought Christianity to the world through the first apostles, who proclaimed the resurrection of Jesus Christ, the gifts of His Holy Spirit, the power over sin and Satan, the full redemption plan and forgiveness of God for every human being by the blood sacrifice of God himself on Calvary.

Through this one family, the family of Jacob, we have the knowledge of the reality of heaven (as Jesus taught it and through John's account in Revelation) and the promise of the Savior's return. In fact, for the first ten years of Christianity, Jacob's descendants were the only ones who proclaimed the Gospel of Jesus to the world. Christianity was reserved for Jacob's kids until God instructed Peter to tell Cornelius, a Gentile, that God does not show favoritism, and that the message God sent to the children of Israel was for all people. (Acts 10.)

When Gentiles became believers, Christianity was birthed into the world and the task of spreading the Good News went beyond the limits of this one family. But for the 1,800 years before Jesus came, Jacob's kids were the only witnesses of God coming to live in man. This means no one believed in Christ besides Jacob's family until Peter shared God's truth with the Italian centurion years after the church was birthed at Pentecost.

Through faith in Jesus Christ, Luke the physician, a Gentile, became Jacob's spiritual descendant. Luke wrote the dynamic record of the book of Acts, which reveals the Holy Spirit to the present-day church. If Jacob had not been obedient to God's plan, this wealth of knowledge, provision and power which was to come through his family would have been delayed while God looked for someone else through which to reveal His plan.

We can be thankful that Jacob and Joseph faithfully applied the principles of ruling, gaining and giving when all they had to begin with was their faith in God's promises to them.

All Wealth

When we are diligent to live justly, God will give us more than material wealth. The greatest treasure we will receive is the revelation of God himself. God is at work to bless mankind, and He desires a personal relationship with us. He will invite us to be a part of His plan, but when He does we face the crisis of whether or not we believe His Word to us. If we believe God wants us involved in His work, there is always an adjustment to make in our lives.

Some of us may be asked to change our thinking and renew our minds. Some of us may be called to physically move from one place to another. Some of us will need to begin ruling over our circumstances. Some of us will need to serve in the task before us, as Jesus would serve if the opportunity were His. Some of us may be called to give more or administrate care to needy people. Whatever the call is, we will experience the reality of God when we see Him move in response to our obedience.

God is the rewarder of those who diligently seek Him. (Heb. 11:6.) God reveals Himself to those who obey His Word and who walk in right standing. We can see that He blessed Abraham, Jacob and Joseph for administrating His wealth for the care of His people. He blesses all who trade and tithe in order to offer their gain for His kingdom work.

The Neglected Keys of Financial Success

You now have my summary of the neglected keys to divine financial success. I share even more details on how to acquire and maintain great wealth in the many teaching tapes you can obtain by writing to my ministry address in the back of this book.

In the next few chapters, I will share with you specific ways to apply the threefold principles we have discussed so far. For many years, I was dedicated to giving, but I had no plan to replenish my source for giving. I couldn't understand where my "hundredfold return" was that is promised to righteous givers. When I asked God to show me what was wrong, He revealed to me that I had no plan to gain back an increase after I had given my seed money away. You can learn to apply the principles of gaining and giving by ruling over what has been entrusted to you and enjoy an immediate, abundant gain.

12
Applying the Principles
to Receive Flowing Wealth

Those who succeed in ministry are not only great givers, but they also apply sound business principles of gaining an increase and managing their finances for the Lord's work.

I had to overcome unscriptural, religious thinking in order to begin operating my ministry with biblical business principles. In September of 1990 God showed me that I had a responsibility to share these overlooked principles with the body of Christ, to encourage financial success for use in God's work.

To my knowledge, no one is teaching the church the Principle of Gaining by Trading for financial success. This is the premeditated plan of gain by the sale of one's goods and services for profit in order to generate wealth to fund the work of the kingdom. Giving and wise management are being taught, but the wealth-generating plan of God is being ignored.

I saw that successful national ministers were practicing all the principles, but they were not teaching them. I realized that I was teaching them, but not practicing them in my own life.

Selling Tapes, Bibles and Books

Before understanding God's plan of increase for all of His children, it was difficult for me to sell anything that related to our ministry. I never had peace about charging for our books or tapes, because they are full of information I want to *give* to people. But the lack of peace to sell does not come from God, even though I thought it did.

Many people make decisions by judging whether they have peace or not. As a general rule, it is good to assume that being in the will of Lord results in peace, not turmoil. Yet there was a time when I had a bad feeling about the baptism of the Holy Ghost and the gifts of the Spirit being for today. I thought bad feelings were a warning from God. *My true peace to accept the great gifts of the Holy Spirit came by the truth of God's Word.* His written truth eliminated the unrest I felt when I first began to hear that the power and gifts of the Holy Ghost were for today.

The doubt you may feel toward gaining by trading must be eliminated the same way—by the truth of God's Word.

Renew the Mind with the Word of God

Several years ago, I frequently ministered in a Pentecostal church over a period of several months. The crowds were increasing on the one night a week I ministered there. Finally God showed me to begin teaching that God wants His people to prosper. Immediately, the crowds dropped eighty percent after I announced I would be teaching about prosperity for several services.

The people stopped coming because they had bad "feelings" against prosperity. They had been taught that it is not spiritual to prosper. They thought prosperity was from the devil, and because they had a bad *feeling* about prosperity, they thought the unrest was from God. They had not been taught the truths of God's Word about His will to prosper them. The bad feelings were from the devil, who was trying to keep God's truth from working in and for believers. Feelings are not the barometer we are to use to test God's will.

To the twenty percent of the Pentecostal congregation who reluctantly came to hear the truths of prosperity, I shared the following:

"Let me give you an example of how sometimes we base our beliefs on what we have been taught, instead of on what God's Word actually says. I was raised in an Evangelical church, as some of you were.

"What do you think would happen if, when asked to teach there, I announced my subject would be about the baptism of the Holy Ghost with the evidence of speaking in tongues, the nine gifts of the Spirit being for today, and the responsibility of all believers to cast out devils, to lay hands on the sick and expect the sick to recover?

"Let me ask you how many people from the Evangelical church you think would show up to hear me preach these great truths of the Bible that you know are vital and powerful truths of God for all people?

"You know that there would only be a few of the members of the Evangelical church, if any, who would come to hear what the Word of God has already revealed to you as truth. You have settled this matter by God's written Word and you have received these precious gifts in your life.

"You know that your Evangelical brothers and sisters in the Lord need to hear the truths of the power and healing of God. You know they cheat themselves, others and dishonor God if they reject His truth concerning His power for them. You know the benefits of the Holy Spirit, who is ready to empower them for advancing His kingdom to others, because you have experienced the wonderful fellowship of His presence. You can see that they would be wrong to give way to the bad feelings against these truths of the Holy Ghost's power, which they have been taught is not for today.

"Many of us who have received the Holy Spirit since we believed (Acts 19:1-7) had the same bad feelings when first we heard these truths, because we had been taught against them. When the truth was evident to us in God's Word, we overcame the feelings against the truth and received God's blessing of fellowship through the Holy Spirit."

Prosperity Is an Evangelical Teaching

I could announce in the Evangelical church in which I was raised that I would be teaching on prosperity, and the church members would flood in with expectant rejoicing. They have already accepted many of the truths of prosperity. They have not been taught against these truths; therefore they have a good and expectant feeling about God's desire to bless His people.

It is time for the whole church to mature and grow in the truth and power of the Word of God. Pentecostals can grow in knowledge of God's prosperity, and Evangelicals can grow in the knowledge of His ministry gifts and power to heal.

When I announced my intent to teach on prosperity at the Pentecostal church, the exact same thing happened there that happens in the Evangelical church when I announce that I will teach about the Holy Ghost. No one shows up with expectancy and excitement, and the people who do come seem hesitant and guarded. This happens because some truths of God's Word have been taught against for years. *God's provision for prosperity and power should be taught as valuable treasures for today.*

Satan has deceived many Evangelicals to believe the Holy Ghost's power has passed away, and he has tricked many Pentecostals into believing prosperity is worldly. Then he separated the church so one group of believers would not encourage and build up another with their testimony of God's truth in their lives. We are encouraged in Hebrews 10:24,25 NIV to **consider how we may spur one another on toward love and good deeds. Let us not give up meeting together, as some are in the habit of doing, but let us encourage one another—and all the more as you see the Day approaching.**

Praise God for the Evangelicals! Praise God for the Pentecostals! Above all, praise God when the truth and the power of the name of Jesus is believed by all of His people! The truth sets us free (John 8:32) to hold to the teachings of Jesus Christ, making us truly His disciples. Truth keeps us prosperous and whole to serve Jesus—the One who loved us and gave Himself for us.

The Truth About Ice Cream

Because of my heart toward children, I could never own a business of selling ice cream, candy, snow cones or anything else kids love to eat. Perhaps I could handle being a clerk in someone's grocery store, but I could not be in the business of making and selling ice cream to kids for a profit. My heart cries from deep within me with a mushy, highly sentimental argument, "I can't *charge* kids for ice cream! I want to *give* ice cream to kids."

I have also had nearly the same heartrending feelings toward putting a price on my teaching tapes and books, arguing "I just can't put a price on spiritual things!" I just couldn't sell someone a Bible. I felt like this was not a spiritual thing to do, and I have been tormented with feeling like I shouldn't or couldn't sell anything to anybody, anytime. I want to be a good witness and just give everything away, including ice cream.

It was also difficult for me to ask people to be partners with us and pledge to our ministry. I just did not feel like this was the spiritual thing to do. Repeatedly I could easily give, but I couldn't believe it was scriptural to gain by trading or to ask people to support our ministry. Instead, I would go to work for someone else in order to support our ministry, rather than obey the principle of gaining to give and giving to gain! But whenever I went to work for someone else, it was difficult to have time for our ministry.

The Lord showed me that *unless someone had been willing to put aside the sentimental notion to give ice cream away instead of charge for it, the world could never have ice cream.* Children would not have an unlimited supply of ice cream unless someone had applied the biblical principle of marketing a good product for a fair profit.

The World's Richest Man Can't Give Away Ice Cream

The richest man in the world could not give everyone ice cream, even one time. There are 5 billion people in the world today and the world's richest man is worth 15 billion dollars. You may think that would make it possible for him to give each person in the world $3.00 worth of ice cream. Not so! He would have the money for a serving of ice cream for each person, but he would not have the billions of dollars needed to pay for transportation and all related expenses to get the refrigerated product to all the remote places where the people are.

Even if he did accomplish this feat at least once, he could not do it again. This totally charitable deed would deplete his billions of dollars and leave him with debt. The rich man whose unselfish desire was to give ice cream to the people of the world would now be totally devastated financially and emotionally, and people would have a greater taste for something they couldn't have again. The world still would not have ice cream, and the kind-hearted man could not do anything about it except wish for another opportunity.

I have experienced this devastating position several times in the past. I can assure you that the desire to give is lessened by the frustrations of the terrible crisis situation that results when you give away everything you have without a plan to regain what has been given away.

Be Dedicated to Both Gaining and Giving

To only be motivated by the desire to give the world ice cream (or whatever product is in your heart to share with others) and never apply the divine principle of *fair profit* is to deny the world ice cream.

The Lord showed me from His Word why I could not give like I wanted to. To violate the plan to gain is to deny the world an unending supply of what He gives you for the world. To operate the principle of gaining (or profit) guarantees God's *unending* supply as the principle of giving guarantees God's *protected* supply.

God promises divine material protection when we tithe from our increase and give.

> **Will a man rob God? Yet ye have robbed me. But ye say, Wherein have we robbed thee? In tithes and offerings.**

> **Ye are cursed with a curse: for ye have robbed me, even this whole nation.**

> **Bring ye all the tithes into the storehouse, that there may be meat in mine house, and prove me now herewith, saith the Lord of hosts, if I will not open you the windows of heaven, and pour you out a blessing, that there shall not be room enough to receive it.**

> **And I will rebuke the devourer for your sakes, and he shall not destroy the fruits of your ground; neither shall your vine cast her fruit before the time in the field, saith the Lord of hosts.**

> **Malachi 3:8-11**

How to Give to the World

Whether it is in your heart to share ice cream, Bibles or your service, you must reject the sentiment to only give away your product. It is difficult when your desire to give away your "ice cream" is born out of a pure heart for God, but you must apply the *purity of God's principle for consistent supply.* You must produce and market your product or service for a profit and then give God the firstfruits of the increase—wisely give, wisely gain, then wisely maintain. If you don't, the world will never have your ice cream, Bibles, tapes or anything else you desire them to have.

You must obey God's principles to be used to fill the earth with the glory of His abundant supply. Refusing to charge for the product because you want to give to the world is to rob the world of what you have to give. Refusing to apply the principles of trading to gain and gaining to give will prevent you from giving the world what is in your heart for them to receive.

Don't Rob the World

Don't rob people by robbing yourself. Give them the fullness of what you have by marketing your goods and services for fair profit. Your obedience to gain a profit from selling will enable you to give the world what was impossible for you to give before. Fully obey God!

- Gain and give!
- Give and gain!
- Increase and maintain to gain and give!

This is God's way, as taught by Jesus and as seen in the examples of the forefathers of our faith. Don't let feelings stop you from doing what God's Word clearly tells you to do. Don't just ask God for money, also ask Him for ideas. He has already given you talents and faith as your seed with which to begin.

13

How to Begin

Scripture clearly instructs Christians to witness and win people to Jesus. Witnessing is not an option. We don't need to ask God if He wants us to tell others about Jesus. Scripture settles this. Our prayer must be, "Dear Lord, how do I win them? And how do I go about witnessing to the individual persons with whom I am in contact?"

Scripture clearly instructs Christians also to gain and then give from the increase to the work of the Lord. Gaining is not an option. Every Christian has been given the continual commission to witness and to gain.

Just as you press toward the goal of being an *active witness* for Jesus, you must move on toward the goal of becoming an *active gainer* for His work. The steps you take for witnessing are the same ones you take to gain financial increase, financing your ability to reach others with your ministry.

Pray

Begin your act of obedience with prayer. As you go before God in prayer, base your prayer on the Word of God. You now know it is scriptural to gain by trading, so ask God how you should gain an increase for His work. He is always ready to show you ways to be an effective witness, and He will show you what abilities you have that people need. He will give you the ideas, methods and the desire to obey His Word on gaining. Pray a prayer to Him like this: *Lord, give me the ideas, methods and the desire to obey Your Word concerning Your Principle of Gaining by Trading. Show me how to acquire and learn the technical and financial skills that I need to be an effective business person for You. In Jesus name I pray. Amen!"*

Learn

Learning to be an effective business person in finance and marketing does not come automatically, and knowing how to win people to Jesus does not come automatically. But God will work in us to perfect us for the work He has called us to do.

Jesus said to Andrew and Peter, **Come ye after me, and I will *make* you to become fishers of men** (Mark 1:17). The statement, "I will make you to become..." very emphatically implies that if you follow Jesus, He will *build* you into what you are not. Follow Him and He will create in you what He wants you to be! Jesus said that He will make you to become a fisher of men.

To become skilled and effective in witnessing, we must pray and submit to Christ's command to go! We must learn to develop what God expects of us. We must learn to be skilled gainers and maintainers, because He wants us to be *gainers of wealth as well as fishers of men*. Gaining and maintaining must be learned because **poverty and shame shall be to him that refuseth instruction** [principles of learning]: **but he that regardeth reproof shall be honored** (Prov. 13:18).

If we obey God by learning to be effective gainers and soulwinners, we honor Him. Then reproof is replaced with, **Well done, good and faithful servant! You have been faithful with a few things; I will put you in charge of many things. Come and share your master's happiness!** (Matt. 25:23 NIV).

It's Always Time to Witness

Many people hesitate when they could witness for the Lord. They say they are waiting for a specific word or special feeling from God before they will actively tell someone about Jesus. In waiting for this specific direction or special feeling from God before you will witness, you end up not witnessing very often, if ever.

The Word says we are to be a witness to *every* creature. We have God's spoken Word from His written Word. What He wants us to do is clear and to whom we are to witness is also clear. We don't need another revelation from Him about whom to witness to when we have His written Word concerning it. To wait to hear from God before you will witness makes you a very ineffective and inconsistent witness.

It's Time to Make Money Work for God's Purposes

When you hesitate and wait for another revelation about making money for the Lord's work, your ineffectiveness is the same as when you hesitate to witness. You don't have to hear a verbal command from God when you have His written Word on what to do. Scripture clearly teaches that consistently making money with honest principles of trade is part of His financial plan of plenty for all people.

I have often met dedicated Christian people who doubt whether or not to get a job or sell a product because they want to hear specifically from God before they go to work or do anything to generate money for their support. They feel that faith means to totally depend on God for the things they need. They fear they will be out of God's will if they don't have a special spiritual encounter with God to tell them whether to work or not.

When they use all the money they have saved, many of them will borrow all they can. Still, they are waiting for a specific word from God before they will do something to make money. At some point in time, creditors will not loan them any more money. Then they begin to sell off what they own in order to live while they wait to hear from God. Often they reach a desperate and frustrating place of being without money and without the word they needed from God.

In this financial disaster of not having money with which to eat or pay the bills, they finally accept any honest way to make money in order to survive. By then, the job is often a low-paying clerk's position or hard labor task which most other people do not want.

These Christians who have so earnestly waited to hear from God before working are now happy and relieved to have this low-paying, menial position. Yet they still have not specifically heard from God! This least desirable of jobs is a ray of hope to bring them out of the financial mess they are now in, a mess caused because they wanted to hear from God before they would do anything to make money.

Does God Let His Children Down?

God did not let these Christians down. He did answer them. He told them He would bless *all the work of their hands* (Deut. 28:1,2,8,12). God put Adam in the garden of Eden to work it and take care of it. (Gen. 2:15.) He has never told His children not to work. Instead, He promised to bless all those who faithfully put their hand to the job.

> The Lord will send a blessing on your barns and on everything you put your hand to. The Lord your God will bless the land he is giving you.

> The Lord will open the heavens, the storehouse of his bounty, to send rain on your land in season and to bless *all the work of your hands*. You will lend to many nations but will borrow from none.

> **Deuteronomy 28:8,12 NIV**

God Gives Us Great Liberty

Adam had only one restriction in the garden, and He did not have to keep seeking God to see if He had changed His mind. He knew that he was never to partake of the one forbidden tree. God's Word was absolute and His "No!" never meant that someday it would be permitted.

Adam also had God's approval to enjoy everything else in the garden. Tremendous liberty was granted to Adam to do whatever he wanted to do, as long as he stayed away from the one forbidden tree that represented rebellion against the abundant life that God had planned for him.

God grants us the same freedom to choose what we want to do each day, as long as we obey the written instructions He has already given us in His Word. The *yeses* far exceed the *nos* in God's plan for us, just as God told Adam that he could partake of *every* tree in the garden that was pleasant to the sight and taste, except the one forbidden tree. (Gen. 2:16,17.)

It was not necessary for Adam to intently seek God before he could partake of all the things God had already granted him to enjoy. Freedom to partake of all the exceeding good things of the garden was God's will for him. Another yes from God was never necessary, because His Word meant yes!

Whether individuals should work or not should be settled by what the Word says. The Word clearly teaches that God will bless *all you put your hand to do*. If God is going to bless the work we do, we should certainly expect to gain an increase from our labor.

Thinking you must have a verbal approval or "a witness of the Spirit" is to doubt what the Word says. To receive God's blessing on our work, we must believe and not doubt God's promises and commandments. The main requirement for being blessed in all you do is to know that *you must hearken diligently to what the Word of God says.*

Hearing God's Voice

As Christians, with the Spirit of God dwelling within us, we definitely know when God says no to something we want to do. We usually lose our sense of peace when we consider proceeding with a plan that God has definitely told us not to carry out. We enjoy the peace of God when we obey His instructions.

He has clearly directed us in His Word to multiply and increase from the work of our hands and the witness of our testimony. We are to obey His Word in witnessing and in making money. God may redirect us on our approach to working and witnessing, but He has definitely told us that we should be doing *both*.

If the approach you are using consistently leaves you frustrated with a negative result, God may be saying no to the way you are witnessing or the work you have chosen to do. To go against His no is to insure hardship and failure.

God rarely repeats in an audible voice what He has already told us in His written Word to do. If you insist on hearing a *verbal word* from God before you do something to make money, *you will not do much.*

Proceed with your plans to make money as long as God doesn't clearly show you to stop, then proceed with expectancy. God is able to speak to your heart, and He will not let you fall if you are trusting in Him to guide you. God's approval of your work is based on His written Word, promising to bless the work of your hands and to fill your storehouses.

Another Example of Our Liberty to Prosper

God told Joshua to study His laws and meditate on them day and night. By keeping His Word in our heart, it is easier to know His will concerning our plans. God promised Joshua prosperity and success when he kept the commands

God had given him. This is an important principle in the foundation of our success formula of God's Plan for Flowing Wealth.

> **This book of the law shall not depart out of thy mouth; but thou shalt meditate therein day and night, that thou mayest observe to do according to all that is written therein: for then thou shalt make thy way prosperous, and then thou shalt have good success.**
>
> **Have not I commanded thee? Be strong and of good courage; be not afraid, neither be dismayed: for the Lord thy God is with thee whithersoever thou goest.**
>
> **Joshua 1:8,9**

God said in these two verses that we make our own ways prosperous and have good success when we observe to do what His written Word says to do. God is with us wherever we choose to go. This is the same liberty He gave Adam. The principles are the same for all of us who are in Christ.

We don't have to have definite direction on which tree to partake of or which direction to go to make money or to witness. The command is to *go into all the world*. We are to start from where we are and be fruitful from where we are until all the world is reached.

If God says no to the approach you are using, then do it another way until He does not say no. But find a way to sell your services or products for a profit to finance your call to be a witness, for God has said yes to the task in His Word.

Do Not Be Dismayed

It is very important to know what *dismayed* means. God not only told Joshua to be *courageous* and to *not be afraid*, but He also told him to *not be dismayed*. To be *dismayed* is to not know what to do. The word suggests *fear or discouragement at the prospect of some difficulty or problem which one does not quite know how to resolve because of his lack of understanding.*

When David came to where Saul's troops were cowering before the challenges of Goliath, the giant Philistine warrior, he found them *dismayed* and terrified. (1 Sam. 17:11.) For forty days the armies of God were fearful before the boisterous challenge of the giant, and they did not know what to do.

David was not fearful or dismayed. He immediately knew what to do. He knew his rights by knowing the Word, that he and all of God's obedient people could immediately stop the bullying attack and opposition of any enemy. He knew this uncircumcised Philistine had no right to defy the armies of the living God. (1 Sam. 17:26.)

Though the challenge seemed great, David took the giant's head off that very day. To be dismayed is to not know your rights, rights that give you the authority to solve a conflict. David knew his rights and exercised his authority immediately. To not exercise your rights of authority is to be dismayed. Victory is delayed when you are dismayed, because you do not know you have rights from God to win in your daily life.

When God Says No

If you are a person who consistently prays and waits before God, you will know if He is saying no to you before you even start. He doesn't play games with us, letting us invest time and money and then saying no when we would lose everything. God will give direction before the deal, if you seek His direction. The time to seek His voice is before you begin a business deal, not after you have signed a contract.

For several years I entered into business deals wondering if God would bless me through the opportunity. I was dedicated to serving God, yet often trouble would arise and I would lose instead of gain. I entered business negotiations thinking, *I know God wants to bless me, but I wonder if this is the plan through which He will prosper me? I wonder if He will let me win or lose in this deal?*

Most of the time, I did not prosper in the situations I entered into with doubts and questions in my mind. I lost, because to *wonder* is to be *dismayed*. To wonder and be dismayed is to not believe God's Word. *Belief* is a requirement necessary for receiving what God's Word promises.

In each unsuccessful business deal, I had not believed God would bless me the way His Word says He will. I was wondering, *Will He?* To wonder is to be curious yet doubtful, and it is not faith in His Word. Wondering is doubting His Word, which says He *will* bless and He has not said no to prospering His people.

In order to bless me while I was wondering, God displayed His mercy toward me. The times I succeeded when my mind was full of doubt were not because I believed His Word said He would bless me. God's *mercy* kept food on my table. But there was not the abundant blessing His Word promises we are to have.

A Personal Example of Dismay

For many years I had tried to sell a particular oil deal. People did not seem to be interested, because it wasn't near proven production or existing oil and gas wells. At various times over a fifteen-year period, I tried to get people interested. My main reason was, I just *knew* oil and gas were there. The more I worked with the deal, the more expenses I incurred. By the time fifteen years had passed, I was ministering full-time with a growing family and I needed extra money.

I had renewed interest from oil men in Dallas, but they had delayed for months trying to make up their minds. There were still questions because there were no close wells to encourage anyone to take the deal.

Finally the landowner who had so patiently worked with me through the years said, "David, if your men don't take the deal by a certain day at noon, I will take this offer to the people whom I now have interested." I had less than a week to close my sale or else lose fifteen years of labor and money.

I began to seriously seek God. Again I wondered why God had not blessed me in my fifteen-year attempt to sell this oil deal. His Word said He would bless and prosper us if we serve Him and *believe*. I had been serving God with all my heart and I thought I was believing His Word. Yet I was beginning to feel greatly disappointed in God for not blessing me as His Word promises.

As I sought Him and asked Him what the problem was, He showed me that I had not believed He would bless this deal or any deal I ever went into. I was always wondering, *Will He bless this? His Word says He will bless when we put Him first, but will He bless this? I know it is His will for me to work, but will He let me make some money, or am I in this just to be a good witness to those I am in contact with?* I would wonder, *Maybe a good attitude in losing is what God wants me to show to others as I lose.* I would think, *Whatever Your will is, God, that's what I want. I want Your perfect will in my life, and if losing will advance Jesus more by my life of loss, then that's what I want, God.*

The Problem Was Doubt and Dismay

I was not taking God at His Word. I was *wondering* instead of *believing*. To wonder is to be dismayed. To be dismayed is to not believe the exactness of God's Word. To not believe the exactness of His Word is to guarantee loss, unless He moves in mercy to bless your unbelieving efforts.

I had less than twenty-four hours to do something different, or fifteen years of repeatedly losing on the same deal would be a permanent loss. The landowner would not let me try again. After all, fifteen years is a long time for a fellow to have patience with a person, don't you agree?

When the Lord showed me in Joshua 1:8 what dismay meant and that it guaranteed loss, I immediately made a correction in my thinking. I showed my wife, Suzie, what the Holy Spirit had revealed to me about the meaning of dismay and that *I had been losing because of my doubt and unbelief.*

She was excited. We had a very short time to put our new ingredient of "sure success" to work. The new ingredient was "confidence," based on what God's Word says is your right to prosperity, providing He has not said no at the beginning of your business plan.

Remember to Seek God First

The time to question God is at the first of a deal. If you don't learn to seek Him before you begin, Satan has a greater opportunity to mess you up on most of your deals. The devil prefers to interfere after you have already spent time and money on your plan. If you don't give God a chance to say no before you enter a business deal, you will think He is telling you no when you encounter trouble in your business transactions.

God isn't the One who is saying, "I want you to lose on this deal. Be a good witness now, and let everybody else make on this but you. Show them what a good Christian you are by being willing to lose."

I can assure you, if God is the One who says no, He will tell you before you begin. This is why it is important to seek His voice before you go into something. If God doesn't tell you no, then you will know who your opposition really is when you encounter trouble in the deal. You will recognize when Satan is trying to cause you to lose again and rob you of your promise of prosperity from God.

If you are not sure who your opposition is, you will allow trouble to get rid of you instead of using the power and wisdom of God to get rid of trouble. If you wonder if it is God who said "No! You need to lose; I will bless you some other time," you will falter and give way to the enemy who is at work to stop the blessings of God in your life. But you will be able to move on with confidence if you seek God first and know He says in His Word, "I will bless all you put your hands to do, I have not said no to you."

What we believe His voice has said to us must agree with what His written Word says, or else it was not God talking to us. *The voice of God and the Word of God must agree, or it is not God.* The thief comes to kill and destroy God's blessed plans in our lives, but God will not let you lose when you put your confidence in Him. You have confidence in Him to win when you know He has not said no.

Getting Family Agreement

Our two older sons, David and Christian, were six and four years of age at the time I was seeking God concerning this sale. I am not permitted to tell you how old Suzie was, but I asked them to kneel down and believe with me according to this new ingredient of guaranteed success. I explained to them what *dismay* was and that this was where I had been missing consistent financial blessings. I told the boys I would get them the two red Honda Model 40 motorbikes they had been wanting and I told Suzie I would buy her the new living room suite she wanted when the deal came through.

We all believed *dismay* had been our problem, so we asked forgiveness for our sin of unbelief. Then we prayed, believing and thanking God for blessing this business contract. We knew it was His will for us to prosper in this deal, because it was an honest trade and He had not said no.

The Good Deal Zooms Through

With expectant confidence I waited for the phone call, knowing the Dallas oil men would have the lease money to me before the noon deadline the next day. Of course, I had informed them of the time limit.

Before the deadline came, an amazing thing happened. The phone rang a few hours after we had prayed and believed the exactness of God's Word to sell the deal. It was not the oil men from Dallas I was expecting with the money. It was an oil man friend of mine who had looked at this deal several times in past years, but who was never seriously interested before.

He wanted to know if I had sold the deal yet. I told him of the time limit at noon the next day, but that I had oil men from Dallas whom I was sure would take the deal and have the money to me by the deadline a few hours away.

He said to me, "David, if the men from Dallas don't take the deal, I will take it and have the money to you in time for you not to lose the leases."

The Giant is Slain in a Day

David slew the giant in a day by not being dismayed. And in one day of repenting from the deception of my unbelieving, wondering dismay, I also slew "my giant," which had caused me to lose by bullying and challenging me for fifteen years on this one oil deal.

Though my friend wanted the deal, I told him I would give the Dallas people time to bring the money. If they did not, I told him the deal would be his.

Slaying *dismay* gave me two oil companies with the money to take my deal. This all happened the very day I believed *the exactness of God's Word* and put *expectant belief* into practice. This was a result that fifteen years of

163

dedication to God with *wondering* instead of *exact belief* could not produce.

I made thousands of dollars on the day of the deadline, which was less than twenty-four hours from the time we prayed with *expectant belief*, not wondering doubt! I retained an overriding interest, which means I am paid for a certain part of what the wells produce without having to pay any expenses to drill or operate the wells. Two wells have been producing for several years now. More will be drilled. Each will pay us throughout the life of the wells with no expense to us, ever.

All of this came about by believing what God's Word had said all along. The demon of doubt, called Dismay, could no longer taunt us with the religious-sounding whisper, "Losing for Jesus is the righteous thing for you to do." We now knew the truth and the truth set us free to enjoy the provision of God.

God's Financial Truths Produce Cash

This one truth, of seeing the deception of dismay and replacing it with expectant belief to receive what the Word promises, pays me in dollar bills every month. Truth pays! It does not cost. It pays me every month, in cash. I receive a check from the oil company every month. I look at it as payment for applying God's truth with Suzie and the boys. We were certain to lose in this deal before the Holy Ghost revealed the meaning of God's written truth.

God's truth pays in dollar bills, because much of God's truth teaches He will prosper our storehouses (increase our finances). Believe His truth and apply the Principle of Expectant Belief to put His financial blessing in your possession.

Get Technical Help

There are many good books on how to own and operate your own business. Go to the business section of a local bookstore or library and begin to equip yourself to be an effective business person. *Entrepreneur* magazine is an excellent resource which will inspire and inform you. This publication also offers short and thorough courses on how to become successful in business with your products and services.

The Small Business Administration has many publications on almost all aspects of most types of businesses. Check your phone book or ask for more information concerning their services through your local library.

We have a series of 400 plus tapes on *The Biblical Principles of Marketing Your Goods and Services for Great Profit* which would help and inspire you in developing your business. You can buy these individually or save by buying in quantity. We also would be happy to recommend several books and courses if you will call or write to us. (Easy ordering information is in the back of this book.)

Finally, always remember these principles:

• Financial loss is not God's way.

• To gain and give is God's way.

• To lose, for the purpose of witnessing, is a deception of Satan.

• To gain and give advances the kingdom of God and bears witness of Jesus Christ which cannot be denied!

14
Wealth Can Be Yours

For many years, I did not know of these biblical principles which I have shared with you in this book. But early in building my business career, the following Bible verse stirred my faith in a dynamic way.

A good man leaveth an inheritance to his children's children: and the wealth of the sinner is laid up for the just.

Proverbs 13:22

I had been self-employed in the oil and equipment business for about six years before I began to live the life God wanted me to live. During those early years, I repeatedly gained and lost a great amount of money because I was not serving God. Everything went wrong "honey-wise" and "money-wise" until I began to obey God's call on my life. This included surrendering to preach His Gospel, which I had previously refused to do.

I could not live the Christian life fully until I learned that the power of the Holy Spirit is available for us today as it was for the early Christians, whose experiences are recorded in the book of Acts. Since Jesus baptized me with the Holy Ghost, it has been easy to live the life of faith.

John the Baptist spoke of this experience in John 1:33: **And I knew him not: but he that sent me to baptize with water, the same said unto me, Upon whom thou shalt see the Spirit descending, and remaining on him, the same is he which baptizeth with the Holy Ghost.**

Jesus explained to the disciples how the Holy Spirit lived with them but would one day be in them in John 14:15-18:

> If ye love me, keep my commandments. And I will pray the Father, and he shall give you another Comforter, that he may abide with you for ever; Even the Spirit of truth; whom the world cannot receive, because it seeth him not, neither knoweth him: but ye know him; for he dwelleth with you, and shall be in you. I will not leave you comfortless: I will come to you.

After receiving the power of the Spirit (Acts 1:8), I began to beg God to let me preach and use me any way He wanted. It was impossible for me to live right before the power of the Holy Spirit came into my life; I had absolutely refused to ever be a preacher.

As I began to live the just and pleasing life God wanted me to live, I still owed a great amount of money. I wanted to get out of debt as quickly as possible so I could enter full-time ministry, but I needed to sell a lot of big equipment in order to be free of my debts. I had no working capital for resaleable equipment, and my bankers could do no more to help me. They were willing to loan enough money to keep food on our table, but not enough for me to purchase the equipment for resale. I could not get out of debt until I had money with which to trade and gain.

Confidence to Win

I thought I was doing everything God had commanded me to do, and I tried to put God first in every area of my life. I paid my tithes. I gave, gave, gave. I went to every church service I could find to go to. I studied the Word, fasted, prayed, witnessed and listened to religious radio stations all the time. I played sermon tapes on a huge reel-to-reel tape recorder whenever I was in my car. It took up most of the front seat, and 8-inch preaching tapes were everywhere in my company car. (This was before the cassette recorder days.)

I heard the Word in power everywhere I went. As I pulled up to oil rigs and production companies to sell equipment, my 1965 red Buick "Wild Cat" field car vibrated with the Word and songs of God. The power sounds of God shook my travelling red office just like the present low-rider woofers pulsate down our highways today.

As I left for work each day, so richly equipped with the Word and power of God, I was confident I would make the big money that was needed to set me free of debt so that I could preach full time. Because I didn't have big equipment to sell, I trusted God to lead me to the customers who would buy what I could supply.

I went to those who needed pipe, tanks and other related oil equipment. I found out what they needed to complete their oil wells. Then I asked them to wait before making a final decision on purchasing their equipment until I could give them a bid on all or part of what they needed. I asked them to give me an opportunity to save them money on equal or better equipment. Then I quickly searched for their needs from my various wholesale sources out of the immediate territory, to see what good deals I could make for my customers and for me.

An Old Sinner with Wealth

I knew a man who was a shrewd and successful business person in the equipment and oil business. He had much of the equipment I needed to fill my customers' orders. He had been helpful by selling merchandise to me at a low cost, making it profitable for me to sell at prices that could still save my customers money.

Since I was limited in operating capital, the greatest help this man gave me was to hold my check for the equipment until I delivered it and collected the payment for what I sold. He offered to sell this equipment to me on credit, but I told him I wanted to keep business on a cash basis as nearly as possible. Since I did not have cash, holding my check was the quickest for me to pay him.

I had determined never to buy and sell on a credit basis again, which was the reason for my debts and lack of cash in the first place. Many people I had sold to in the past could not pay me. I had attributed my business failure to not serving God, but there was no cash because people who owed money to me could not pay. It's easy to sell anything on credit, but collecting is something else. I had sold a great amount on credit, and it was a great amount that I could not collect. So, it was not selling but involuntary charity which put me in a position of almost needing charity myself.

Tempted with Loss

The wealthy equipment man who helped me by holding my check was honest and fair, but he was a sinful man. He drank over a fifth of hard liquor a day and first-class cussers would have blushed by the flow of his profane words.

One day when I went to purchase equipment, I found him in his office drunk and depressed. He said, "David, if I could believe that when I die I would just go to sleep, I would take that shotgun and just end it all!" He said this as he nodded toward a double-barrelled shotgun in the corner of the room. I hadn't noticed the shotgun before, because it was propped up in the corner with several fishing rods, which were a common sight in the offices of Texas oil men.

I knew I had to talk to my wealthy sinner friend about Jesus immediately and tell him what the Lord could do for him. I did not want to, but I knew the Word of God says I am obligated to testify to others of God's love for them. I did not feel capable, though. His sinful state seemed too great to accept what I would say about Jesus, that He could help him, forgive him, heal him, deliver him, give him peace, and make him want to live happily and not die.

I was tempted to think, *You can kiss your good deals with him good-bye. If you talk to him about Jesus, he will never hold a check for you again; he will never want you on his property again. Your witness will go over like a lead balloon. It's not wise. You will lose. You are not capable to represent Jesus in a situation as serious as this, with one who is so sinful. You better not! Bye-bye good deal if you talk to him about Jesus!*

I determined that even if it cost me everything, telling him about the saving grace of Jesus was the thing I had to do. His soul and his life were more important than all or any of the business deals in the world. I felt my witness would be weak and feeble. I felt my testimony wouldn't do any good, but I knew telling him of Jesus was the right thing to do. So, in spite of my feelings of inadequacy, I began to tell him about Jesus.

I was right about my witness being rejected and refused. As drunk as he was, he made me look like an utter fool who knew nothing of the power of Jesus. By faith I was witnessing, and by faith I was being intellectually bullied and berated by a drunk man who wanted to committ suicide. He said he didn't even believe in God. I could not sense the presence of Jesus and His power at this battering moment.

Before me stood a swaying, slurring, slobbering, suicidal, life-losing individual who confidently spurted out to me his vast knowledge of all the religions of the world. At that time, I only knew about four denominational names (Baptist, Methodist, Catholic and Pentecostal) but I certainly did not know what they believed. I could not discuss the many religions of the world with him either.

There I stood, religiously illiterate, representing Jesus, demonstrating that I cared about the life of this man who was caught in hopeless despair, and he gave me the intellectual beating of my life. I feebly tried to speak of Jesus and what the Word says He has done for us. I felt useless and powerless, but by faith and not feeling I stood and refused to crumble or leave him to his suicidal intentions.

Finally, I called him by his first name and attempted another approach. I asked him if I could pray for him. I didn't want to pray for him, because I did not like to pray out loud. I certainly didn't feel encouraged to pray out loud in my present lack of confidence, but I knew that praying for him was the right thing to do.

His reply to my caring request to pray for him was, "Nope, I don't want you to pray for me. I respect you and what you stand for, but I don't want you to pray for me. I don't believe in prayer or in God, and I don't want you to pray for me."

His rejection was cold. We parted in a socially polite way—he the dominant one but without Jesus, and I with Jesus, yet apparently beaten. I felt I would never see him again. It seemed evident why there was a well-established policy not to mix religion with business. I had messed up my good deal by standing for Jesus, but to me, trying to help this desparate man was worth the price.

Trying to save this man's life by helping him see the reality of Jesus was the right thing to do. I knew God would bless me in some other way for sacrificing my good deal to put Jesus first and for attempting to save a hopeless man from the despair of not knowing Jesus, the Prince of Peace.

A Strange Phone Call

For the next few days after witnessing to my business friend, I pondered the unpleasant details of the defeating encounter. I determined many times that I had done the right thing, regardless of the end result. I decided that if I could have relived the moment, I would still obey God and witness to him.

I only regretted that I had not been more capable to represent Jesus to my domineering though despairing friend. I had felt like an illiterate fool in presenting the greatness of Jesus. My witness seemed feeble, powerless and apparently unsuccessful.

Then, within a few days of our meeting, I received an unexpected phone call from my friend. His voice was strong and sober as he said, "David, could you come to see me right away? I need to talk to you, as soon as possible!"

My heart leaped with joy and excitement. I could sense that something had happened, something I had not considered possible until this moment. My business friend, who I believed would never want to see me again, was now eagerly asking me to come see him as quickly as possible. I was full of excitement as I drove to his town.

It seemed obvious that he wanted to personally tell me he had accepted Jesus as his Savior and Lord. I anticipated hearing him tell me of his dynamic experience with Jesus and was ready to rejoice with him for knowing his sins were forgiven. It would be wonderful to hear him say that life was now meaningful to him.

As I stepped into his office, he appeared serious and full of comtemplation as he asked me to sit down. Then, with deep concern in his voice, he surprised me again. He did not speak of Jesus.

Instead, he began, "David I have never had a partner in my life. I like the way you operate. You know how to find and sell equipment. You enjoy life and know how to make things happen. I know you have had some business problems. I have money and you don't. I could help you. You could help me. I believe we would make good partners for each other."

Very soberly he continued, "I'll tell you what I would like to do. If you see any equipment, oil wells, oil leases, refineries, or anything else for sale at a price you think would make money, just tell me. We will look it over and submit a bid to buy it.

"I will pay all your expenses and will put up all the money for everything that you think will make money. There's no limit. I'll pay all the trucking, all the legal fees and every type expense we will have. When we begin making profit, I'll give you 42 percent of what we make.

"You can have the freedom to continue in all the other deals you want to on the side. I like the way you operate, David, and I respect you for what you believe. I believe we would make good partners together. What do you think?"

In all this time, I had not said one word. I did not have the opportunity to, for he was talking as fast as he could. I thought, *I wonder if he really means it!* I realized he was stone sober while presenting this fabulous deal to me. I quickly rejected my thought of unbelief and settled with a more hopeful thought of, *We'll see. This sounds too good to be true, but we will see.*

"It sounds great to me," I replied. "I'll start looking immediately."

A Twenty-Well Oil Deal

Two weeks later, I heard about a twenty-well oil deal which was for sale and was open for purchase by submitting sealed bids. I drove to the town, picked up the information package, inspected the deal to see how good the equipment was and then went to my prospective partner.

Together, we thoroughly examined the opportunity, submitted the bid with the required deposit and soon the wells were ours. We made a great amount of money on these wells and my partner did everything that he said he would do and more.

We bought many more oil, gas and equipment deals together and continued to make large amounts of money. I did not provide physical labor or money on any of these deals, and my partner provided me with exactly what he promised, including 42 percent of all the profit we made.

It seemed that money-making opportunities just came to us without even looking for new deals. All of this was happening because I had put God first and was willing to lose in business in order to bring a despairing man to Jesus.

What About My Friend Accepting Jesus?

The Lord directed me to demonstrate the Christian life in front of my partner, but to wait for him to mention the subject of Jesus. As I prayed and continually expected my friend to ask me about Jesus, he would. As we were working on something together, with no one else around, my friend would say, "David, we're gonna talk about this religion business one more time, then we're never gonna mention it again."

He quit drinkng after we became partners and soon after that he accepted Jesus as his Savior. It took from six to nine months for this to happen. During that time, I prayed a great deal and we had many discussions. As I patiently waited on God and let my friend initiate the subject and ask me questions, the Holy Spirit brought him to the reality of Jesus.

What Happened to My Good Deal?

Shortly after my business friend and I became partners, and before he accepted Jesus, I began pastoring a local church in my hometown. The pastor, who was leaving to teach college in another state, and the members asked me to pastor the church. For the next two years, I pastored the church while continuing in the lucrative business God had created for me. I had simply witnessed to a man in a seemingly impossible situation, and God blessed me with the income to get out of debt and gave me an opportunity to preach in a local church.

After pastoring for two years, I felt I was to resign from the church. I went to my partner and told him the Lord had shown me it was time to go into full-time ministry. In order to be a full-time minister of the Gospel, I felt I should have the least amount of material possessions possible. This religious belief so possessed me, I was convinced it would be sinful for me as a minister to have business interests or profit-making, material possessions. I planned to live by faith, so I happily sold out to my partner for a very low price and gave almost everything else away. I traded my big red Buick for the smallest six-cylinder Ford I could find. I planned to live by faith. What deception!

What Happened to Our Wealth?

I was religiously deceived to believe that faith is, "to give it all away." For many years I thought that to be a full-time minister meant that I should be poor and dependent on God to meet my financial needs. Many Christians shared my point of view. Consequently, I continued to give everything away in an effort to serve God.

The Word of God had not told me to give away the provision He had given us. It was quite a revelation to me when years later I realized that Abraham took all his material possessions with him everywhere God led him. I was surprised to discover that he had multiple profit-making businesses wherever he went.

We are told to be like Abraham, the father of faith, and do as he did. He gave to God first, but when others tried to diminish his material possessions, they had a fierce fight on their hands. God backed him up to keep it every time!

Let's *truly* live by faith like Abraham did. Let's learn to use our faith to *keep and increase* material possessions so we can serve God with all our might and wealth. Solomon taught in Proverbs 21:20, **There is treasure to be desired and oil in the dwelling of the wise; but a foolish man spendeth it up.**

The Lord revealed to me the mystery of His will; that is, we are to serve Him by trading for gain and giving from our increase. When I saw what Jesus really taught in Matthew 25 and Luke 19, I changed my perspective to God's perpective and recognized that I had a responsibility to prosper for the Lord and bring my gain to Him for His work.

Since learning that God wants His people to rule over His wealth, we have learned to be faithful over the seed He gives us and to expect an increase with which we can serve Him. We have learned to stop giving all of our seed away, yet we continue to give wisely, and God enables us to give more and more. God has honored His Word to us and is blessing the work we have put our hands to, blessing our increase so that we can serve Him.

As we have shared this teaching with others, we have received exciting testimonies of God's blessing on those who have applied the gaining and giving principles. A friend of mine who is a doctor used to give nearly half of his income away, but he wasn't looking for ways to increase his wealth for God. Now God has revealed to him ways to gain with his money and he gives more from the increase than when he was giving away 40 percent of his income.

When Christians see that Jesus was pleased with the servant who received five talents and came back with five more, they are set free by the truth that God wants His people to prosper. Jesus said to the servant who had gained by trading, **Well done, thou good and faithful servant: thou hast been faithful over a few things, I will make thee ruler over many things: enter thou into the joy of thy lord** (Matt. 25:21).

In other words, blessed are they who have used faith to rule over what is given to them and who increase their wealth for the kingdom. Blessed are those who neither hide their money, nor give it all away, nor waste it, nor lose it (Matt. 25; Luke 19 AP).

Those who learn to rule over wealth will be the good servants who are able to feed the hungry, shelter the stranger, clothe the naked and visit those who are in prison. They will be the ones who are able to do it for the least of the brethren; and, therefore, do it for Jesus (Matt. 25:31-40.)

What Happened to My Friend?

Suzie and I went back to see my ex-business partner several times a year. After six months of not seeing him, his dear wife called and told us that he had peacefully passed away. Knowing he would soon be with the Lord, he had planned his own funeral and had asked his wife to contact me. She repeated one of his last requests to me, "Tell David Wells, I sure would appreciate it if he would preach my funeral."

One of the great joys of my life was the privilege of conducting the memorial service of this friend who once was a despairing sinner, but who became a confident believer by my feeble presentation of Jesus.

The Wealth of the Sinner

Proverbs 13:22b says, **... and the wealth of the sinner is laid up for the just.** My dealings with this friend truly illustrated how the wealth of a sinner had become mine as I demonstrated the just things of God in my business. But more than that—the wealth of God became the wealth of the sinner when the sinner gave his sins to God!

My friend was rescued from his life of sin by coming to a knowledge of God's wealth, as I witnessed and daily illustrated to him how to live the joyous and just life. At the same time, God used the sinner's wealth for me in the business world. This is truly a dynamic fulfillment of this precious promise in Proverbs 13:22, which I did not even know until many years later.

Begin Today

A good man leaveth an inheritance to his children's children: and the wealth of the sinner is laid up for the just.

Proverbs 13:22

Be that good man! Apply God's Plan for Flowing Wealth:

- Gain and Give!

- Give and Gain!

- Leave an inheritance so great it extends even to your children's children!

This is God's way! We have His Word on it!

The wealth of the wicked (sinner) is yours, as you honestly trade your goods and services for it. But tell others of Jesus as you trade your services, so that the wealth of God will also be theirs!

People are hungry for the spiritual wealth of God in Jesus which you have to give them. The reason more people have not believed is because they haven't heard the Good News of God's unconditional love. They simply do not know of His provision for those who are His. As you gain back the material wealth of God, win people for Jesus too. The world is waiting on you, therefore go with your goods, your services—and Jesus!

You have the answer to their needs!

They have yours!

Therefore!

Go!

Trade, Gain and Give!

This is God's divine will, as taught by Jesus.

This is how you can win as you win them!

An Antidote for Financial Failure

Near retirement age, the broken stooped figure of an emotionally and physically shattered man laboriously shuffled through the halls of an asylum. His dreams had been shattered by the weakened national economy, leading to the collapse of the financial empire he had built.

The millions he owed and the impossibility of ever changing the financial ruin of his once vast empire pressed down upon him, reducing him to this frail shell. He pitifully shuffled through the corridors of the institution, suffering through his quiet and lonely recuperation.

From the chapel down the hall he heard people singing, "Be not dismayed, whatever betides; God will take care of you." Suddenly, a truth he learned as a little boy came forcefully to his tired and burdened mind. It was the words of the Master saying, as though personally to him, *Come unto me*, **all ye that labour and are heavy laden, and I will give you rest.** *Take my yoke upon you*, **and** *learn of me*; **for I am meek and lowly in heart: and ye shall find rest unto your souls. For my yoke is easy, and my burden is light** (Matt. 11:28-30).

Feeling he could not take another step because of the weight upon him, this broken man whispered, "Lord, will You help me?" Immediately the load of defeat lifted, and he determined to serve the Lord who had lifted his burden.

Forty-five years later, this same man stood in triumph and strength at an awards banquet, being recognized as one of the most successful businessmen in the history of America. He related the above story, but he was so well-known for mega-success and philanthropy now, it was difficult to imagine he was the broken failure at retirement age so many years ago.

He told of his Formula of Rediscovered Success. It was what the Master had said to him through the Scripture, which burst into his troubled mind in the lonely halls of the asylum so long ago. The three points of success were:

- Come to Jesus.

- Be yoked with Him (Let Him be the boss).

- Learn and apply His teachings (teachings which lead to success in all areas of life, regardless of past failures).

At the time of the awards banquet, J. C. Penney was 95 years of age and still working eight hours a day. He was happy, healthy and successful, as promised in the Divine Formula. This formula worked for J. C. Penney and it will work for you. It is for everyone! The scriptures which penetrated his dark despair and gave him success and happiness are promises to you as well.

Appendix

Keep The Proper Perspective As You Succeed

Can success be measured in money?
Can success be measured in gain?
Can success be measured by fortune?
Can success be measured by fame?

Rich men have died ill-treated,
Paupers though assets quite large,
Alone, forgotten, forsaken—
No love from anyone.

Famous men have died unnoticed,
Lost in the cold halls of fame,
Isolated in mansions of darkness—
No family to share their gain.

Successful are they who have peace in their hearts,
Their family and friends are near,
Trophies of love each day are bestowed,
And they know life for them never ends.

All should reach great fortune!
All should reach great fame!
But success is measured in caring,
And riches in receiving the same!

© David S. Wells III, 1987

About the Authors

David and Suzie Wells have been partners in marriage and ministry since 1969. They are dedicated to helping others learn the principles of successful living.

Suzie believed she was created and destined to marry a minister and be in ministry with him. One night she asked God to reveal to her where the preacher was that she was to marry. She said, "Lord, no young, single ministers are ever sent to our church—only retired, elderly couples. Where is he?"

The Holy Spirit told Suzie the next pastor sent to her church would be single and become her husband. One month later the bishop sent David to pastor Suzie's home church. The first Sunday David was there, Suzie arrived thirty minutes before anyone else. Two months later they were married.

A year passed before Suzie shared with David what the Lord revealed to her about their marriage. They have ministered successfully together for twenty-five years and have three fine sons, David, Christian, and Caleb, who work with them in teaching the principles of victorious Christian living.

David and Suzie are the founding pastors of Redeeming Love Faith Fellowship Church in Abilene, Texas, which has served Abilene and the surrounding Big Country area of Central Texas for more than ten years.

This book is another of their "Maximizing-Success" teachings based on the exactness of the principles of success which Jesus taught. David and Suzie show you how to succeed with power and victory, regardless of your past failures and disappointments. They teach and convince you, according to God's Word, that God wants you to do more than get out of debt. He wants you to prosper exceedingly abundantly above what you could ask or think.

David and Suzie minister extensively in music, the Word, writing and holding "The Dynamics of Successful Living" seminars. Many despairing people in dismal failure (personal and business) have been lifted to high levels of vibrant living and success by what they teach and practice.

For Books,
Tapes and
Exciting Seminars

Call or Write:
David and Suzie Wells
P. O. Box 5646
Abilene, Texas 79608
(915) 692-3664

The Harrison House Vision

Proclaiming the truth and the power
Of the Gospel of Jesus Christ
With excellence;

Challenging Christians to
Live victoriously,
Grow spiritually,
Know God intimately.